Involvement in Learning for Low-Achieving Students

Barbara Smey-Richman

RBS

Research for Better Schools
444 North Third Street
Philadelphia, PA 19123
(215) 574-9300

The work upon which this publication is based was funded in part by the Office of Educational Research and Improvement, U.S. Department of Education. The opinions expressed in this publication do not necessarily reflect the position or policy of the Department of Education, and no official endorsement should be inferred.

Graphic art by Peter Robinson
Word Processing by Bobbi Edwards

This is a product of the RBS Research and Development Project, Keith M. Kershner, Director and the Special Populations Project, Ronald L. Houston, Director.

TABLE OF CONTENTS

PREFACE

The Special Populations Project at Research for Better Schools, Inc. (RBS) has developed a school improvement model to increase the responsiveness of educational programs to the needs of low-achieving students. The model consists of a procedure to assess the support and services provided to these students[1] and resource documents to assist with the implementation of improvements in identified areas of need.

This is one in a series of nine resource documents. Each resource document addresses a separate factor on the "Assessment of School Needs for Low-Achieving Students" survey and contains information that responds to specific survey items. The factors are:

- Student Involvement

- Classroom Management

- Instruction

- Parent Involvement

- Principal Leadership

- School Climate

- School Programs

- Staff Development

- Teacher Expectations

The purpose of the resource document is to review factor-related research and to present implications for teaching practice. Each resource document may be used to support existing school or district strategies to improve educational programming for low-achieving students. Examples of the uses of a resource document include:

- providing the school's task force or planning committee with information for establishing school priorities

---

[1] Assessment of School Needs for Low-Achieving Students: Staff Survey by Francine S. Beyer and Ronald L. Houston; available from RBS.

- serving as a guide for staff development

- serving as a guide for developing student programs (e.g., summer school program, alternative educational program, academic advising program)

- supporting academic advisors, teachers, and other school staff in involving parents of the target group in their children's education.

Resource documents are divided into four sections: (1) review of the problem, (2) teaching implications, (3) summary, and (4) examples of relevant education programs. Each document also includes a list of references.

REVIEW OF THE PROBLEM

For the past two decades, most classroom research concerning low-achieving students has focused on the dynamics of teacher- student verbal interactions and, in particular, on how teachers' beliefs, attitudes, or expectations influence those interactions. Much of this research has used a process-product approach in which relationships are established between measures of teacher behavior (e.g., instructional and classroom management strategies) and student outcomes (e.g., achievement gains, attitudes toward self and school).

Although process-product studies have contributed a great deal, we must also consider that low-achieving students are classroom participants who affect teachers, just as teachers affect them, and that they are actively processing and responding to teacher input. Thus, a complete account of classroom events must include not only information about teacher behaviors (see other resource documents in this series, e.g., Instruction, Classroom Management, Teacher Expectations), but also information about low-achieving students' involvement in learning; that is, how low-achieving students cognitively operate on content in the process of learning and the ways in which the teaching process affects low-achieving students' perceptions, attitudes, and beliefs about themselves and their ability to learn. This shift in focus from teaching events to learning events has been referred to by Winne (1985) as the cognitive mediational paradigm.

Identifying and describing the major characteristics shared by low-achieving students are, by themselves, complex tasks. Research suggests that low achievers are chiefly from the lower strata of society and are disproportionately represented by ethnic minority groups. Labels such as "underprivileged," "educationally disadvantaged" and "culturally disadvantaged" have been used to describe this population; these labels focus on socioeconomic factors (e.g., parents' level of education, family income, availability of reading materials in the home) that have contributed to student difficulties in school. However, due to racial and ethnic sensitivity and, more importantly, the recognition that alienation transcends socioeconomic status (SES), some researchers and educators have begun to describe these youngsters as being "at-risk" of dropping out of school and/or becoming unproductive, underdeveloped, and noncompetitive individuals (Pellicano, 1987, p. 47). Concomitantly, these students put our country at risk of becoming a place inhabited by citizens who are dependent, uncompetitive, and unreactive to market forces.

In recent years, a somewhat different view has caused researchers to go beyond analyzing demographic factors to examining the psychological and behavioral characteristics of the poor achiever. In these studies the term "high-risk" is often used in describing "the individual student's attitudes and behaviors in relation to the educational system by focusing on the probability of his or her academic success or failure" (Blum & Spangehl, 1982, p. 5). This is a significant development, for, unlike the case with socioeconomic factors, educators can have a direct influence over students' academic success or failure and over their perceptions, attitudes, and beliefs about themselves and their schooling. This resource document will focus mainly on three broad psychological/behavioral variables or student characteristics that research has shown to be closely associated with poor academic performance (Blum & Spangehl, 1982). These three variables are cognitive ability, task performance, and attribution of success or failure. This section will conclude with a brief discussion of some key cultural characteristics of low-achieving minority students.

COGNITIVE ABILITY

Many researchers identify poor cognitive ability as a major predictor of low student achievement and lack of persistence within the educational system (Bachman, O'Malley & Johnston, 1978; Beal & Noel, 1980; Bowles & Gintis, 1976; Ekstrom, Goertz, Pollack & Rock, 1986; Gottfredson, 1980; Wehlage & Rutter, 1986). Traditionally, cognitive ability has been measured by intelligence tests that reflect three basic dimensions: the capability to learn, to think abstractly, and to adapt to new situations (Cattell, 1971). The most commonly tested dimension is the ability to think abstractly using mathematical or linguistic symbols.

Critics contend that while intelligence test scores may be relatively accurate in predicting a student's school performance, the tests are concerned with only a limited range of talents. Thus, contemporary educational thought has begun to expand the definition of what constitutes intelligence. For example, Sternberg's (1986b) theory of intelligence describes a triad of interlocking mental abilities, the sum total of which determines a person's intellectual strengths and weaknesses. Those three components of intelligence are the ability to learn from context rather than from explicit instruction, mental flexibility or adaptability to novelty, and insight that finds solutions to problems all at once. Sternberg believes that these components of cognition underlie what we mean by intelligence and are a more accurate gauge of intelligence than the abilities measured by traditional tests.

Like Sternberg, Gardner (1983) also has been in the forefront of the movement to identify various aspects of intelligence and to develop new ways of spotting a child's strengths and weaknesses. Gardner's theory of "multiple intelligence" defines intelligence as "the ability to solve problems or fashion products that are of consequence in a particular cultural setting" (Walters & Gardner, 1985, p. 3). He suggests that there are seven major intelligences in addition to those skills commonly assessed by standardized IQ tests. This list includes: the spatial abilities of the architect; the bodily grace of the superb athlete or dancer; musical gifts; the interpersonal abilities of the great statesman or diplomat; and the inner attunement that allows someone to lead a life by his or her true feelings.

While Sternberg, Gardner, and others are broadening the range of human abilities that make up intelligence, other researchers are questioning the validity of IQ constancy and advocating cognitive modifiability (Ausubel, 1964; Birch & Bortner, 1970; Feuerstein, 1980; Schwebel, 1968). In 1969, the age-old "nature versus nurture" controversy resurfaced when Jensen and others (e.g., Garrett, 1971) advanced the view that innate and largely unmodifiable human limitations were reflected in low IQ scores. Although this debate involves a complex of issues, the two overriding ones are: (1) Are there racial and genetic differences in intelligence? and (2) Is the IQ test a valid tool for measuring intelligence? Critics of the IQ tests and of the concept of intelligence as a static entity (Bronfenbrenner, 1975; Gordon, 1975; Kagan, 1975) cite Skeels and Skodak's (1949) landmark study in support of the positive effects of intervention. Questioning the soundness of Jensen's concept of a "heritability coefficient," Bronfenbrenner concludes that even if such a factor for certain traits does exist, its modifiability is not precluded.

The extent to which intelligence is modifiable has obvious implications for low-achieving students. Some educators (e.g., Blum & Spangehl, 1982; Gordon, 1975) promote the need for special goals for those who have not been adequately prepared for schooling. They urge that these goals should be reflected in a diversity and abundancy of educational experiences, such as alternative schooling models that meet a wide variety of educational needs.

Clearly, improvement in cognitive functioning is one such educational need (Ausubel, 1964; Bruner, 1959). Many researchers believe that thinking can be taught (e.g., Costa, 1985), signaling a new concern in educational psychology with ways to foster "learning-to-learn" abilities (Glaser, 1976), and with the metacognitive behaviors (Brown, Campione & Day, 1981) that enable children to think about their own thinking (e.g., ability to select and understand appropriate strategies; ability to monitor task performance (Presseisen, 1985)). Bruner, in an interview with Hall (1982), identifies this optimistic view of cognitive modifiability as the most promising development in American education during the past decade.

TASK PERFORMANCE

A simple measure of intellectual ability is probably not a sufficient behavioral variable for predicting academic achievement (Sternberg, 1986a, b). Crucial to the new theories of intelligence – even multiple intelligence – is the conviction that task performance depends as much on persistence and willingness to work as it does on cognitive ability. Furthermore, studies show that low-achieving students often lack a concern for accuracy and an active approach to problem solving. These students also demonstrate a penchant for guessing and have difficulty breaking complex problems into a number of simpler ones (Chance, 1986, p. 90). An early study that compared low- and high-aptitude (as determined by an aptitude test) college students on their ability to solve reasoning problems was conducted by Bloom and Broder (1950). These researchers found that the consistency with which the students approached and solved various problems (Whimbey, 1984, p. 68) was of such magnitude that they concluded it was the students' habitual problem-solving style of thinking. For the low-aptitude students, this habitual style was characterized by an indifference toward achieving an accurate comprehension of situations and relationships.

According to Whimbey (1984), Bloom and Broder observed that low-aptitude students were mentally careless and superficial in solving problems. They spent little time considering a question and chose answers based on only a few clues, a feeling, an impression, or a guess. In contrast, high-aptitude students made active attacks on problems. When a question was initially unclear, they often used a lengthy sequential analysis in arriving at an answer. They began with what they understood of the problem, drew on other information in their search for further clarification, and carefully proceeded through a set of steps that finally brought them to a solution.

A number of other researchers have reported similar differences between high- and low-ability students at various age levels and across academic areas (Bereiter & Englemann, 1966; Frankenstein, 1979; Whimbey & Lochhead, 1983). For example, Anderson and colleagues (Anderson, 1981, 1984; Anderson, Brubaker, Alleman-Brooks & Duffy, 1984) observed and then interviewed first graders working on seatwork assignments. Their data indicated that many students, especially low achievers, did not understand the content-related purpose of the assignment or how to undertake the task. Rather than asking for help, the low achievers were content either to respond randomly or to rely on unrelated response sets (e.g., using alternating or geometrical patterns for circling answers on multiple choice assignments, picking a word to fill in the blank in a sentence without first reading the sentence). In addition, the low achievers seemed to be more concerned about completing their assignments than understanding the content. As one said when he finished a worksheet, "I don't know what it means, but I did it" (Anderson, Brubaker, Alleman-Brooks & Duffy, 1984, p. 20). In contrast, high achievers completed most of their assignments successfully and showed less concern about finishing on time.

Another strategy for obtaining insight on cognitive processing differences between high- and low-achieving students is the use of a stimulated recall procedure to analyze teacher-pupil interactions. For example, Peterson, Swing, Braverman, and Buss (1982) showed fifth and sixth graders a videotape of a lesson they had been given and asked them to recall their thought processes at various points in the lesson. Responses showed that low-achieving students were less inclined to attend to the teacher's explanation and were more likely to provide general or imprecise reasons for why they did not understand the lesson. In contrast, high achievers reported using two particular strategies that were modeled or suggested by the teacher: (1) the deliberate return to prior knowledge in order to relate new material to former information, and (2) the use of advance organizers. In addition, the high achievers acknowledged that the teacher's overview promoted their understanding.

Winne and Marx (1982) are particularly concerned with the degree of congruence between teachers' goals for their students' thought processes and the extent to which these processes are successfully elicited. Teacher and student interviews designed to explore teacher intentions and student understanding revealed serious problems in classroom communication. Focusing on teacher behavior, these researchers found teachers to be least successful in engaging students, establishing task definitions, and setting objectives. Furthermore, Brophy (1986a) reported that many teachers are so eager to begin a lesson that they skip over lesson objectives. Only five percent of the teachers Brophy observed explicitly described the purpose of the assignment being presented and even fewer (approximately 1.5 percent) mentioned the explicit cognitive strategies to be used when doing the assignment.

For low-achieving students, the problem of poor classroom communication is complicated by the fact that these students have a difficult time securing relevant information about how academic task systems work. This observation has led Doyle (1982) to conclude that the problems of low achievers should be seen in informational rather than motivational terms. Doyle suggested that from the teaching perspective, low-achieving students need "explicitness, continuity and simplicity to navigate the task systems in the classroom" (p. 532). However, as indicated above, Winne and Marx reported that the ability to provide the guidance and structure so needed by low achievers is also the type of behavior that most teachers are least successful in perfecting.

ATTRIBUTION OF SUCCESS OR FAILURE

The relationship of student perception of ability to academic achievement has been a concern for many cognitive psychologists interested in understanding the factors that influence a low-achieving student's task performance (Bar-Tal, 1978; Covington & Omelich, 1979a, 1979b; Weiner, 1979). The formulations of the cognitive psychologists are guided by attribution theory, which proposes that an individual's interpretation of the causes of success and failure influences future achievement-oriented behavior. One of their most consistent findings is that individuals who believe that the successful completion of a task is due to their own ability will probably attempt similar endeavors in the future because they can expect to do well and feel good about their accomplishments. Conversely, those who believe their achievement is due to other factors, such as luck or ease of assignment, will be less likely to make future efforts. Consequently, ability perception is viewed as mediating or influencing achievement behavior.

One of the original attribution theorists is Rotter (1966) who coined the term "locus of control" to refer to the individual's beliefs regarding personal control over success and failure experiences. Briefly, "internal control" is an individual's belief that an event or outcome is dependent on his or her own behavior or on relatively permanent personal characteristics such as ability. The belief that an event is caused by factors beyond the individual's control (e.g., luck, task difficulty, biased teacher) is labeled "external control."

Attribution theorists have refined and elaborated on Rotter's concept of locus of control. Weiner (1979) claims that effort and ability attributions have different behavioral implications because effort is under the control of the individual and ability is not. Also, ability is generally perceived as a *relatively* stable factor (i.e., it may vary slightly according to situational factors), whereas effort can vary greatly from situation to situation. Hence, Weiner differentiates between two kinds of internal causes of achievement outcomes:

controllable and unstable causes such as effort, and uncontrollable and relatively stable causes such as ability.

The other major difference between Rotter's and Weiner's analyses of achievement-related cognitions is that Rotter emphasizes generalized beliefs (e.g., regarding one's own ability to achieve) that develop with experience in achievement settings and are assumed to hold regardless of situational factors (Stipek, 1982). In contrast, Weiner, although admitting that relatively stable individual differences in perceptions of the cause of achievement outcomes may exist, emphasizes situational factors in the individual's attributional judgments. He claims that students make judgments about causes of achievement outcomes on the basis of information in the current achievement situation (e.g., one may perceive that he/she is competent in short division and not long division or competent in English, but not science). The difficulty of the task, awareness of how others perform, and the student's analysis of his or her own competence at that particular task all interact and exert influence on the subject's judgment of performance. Therefore, as far as Weiner is concerned, past experience in similar achievement contexts is relevant, but it is only one of several factors to be considered.

As compared with Rotter, Weiner's view of the importance of situational factors in formulating attributional judgments is somewhat more optimistic in its implications for low-achieving students (Stipek, 1982). Weiner's theoretical viewpoint suggests that the causal attributions of low-achieving students can be changed, independent of their previous experiences in achievement contexts, by manipulating current environmental factors. Students, for example, can be taught to succeed with more effort or to assess tasks more accurately.

Belief about the roles that success and failure play in achievement behavior has been studied by Dweck and colleagues (Diener & Dweck, 1978; Dweck, 1976; Dweck & Bush, 1976; Dweck, Davidson, Nelson & Enna, 1978; Dweck & Gilliard, 1975; Dweck & Goetz, 1978; Dweck & Reppucci, 1973). They found that some students with a history of poor performance in school persist and actively pursue alternative solutions to a task when they encounter failure, whereas others undergo a marked deterioration in persistence or quality of performance, evidencing what the researchers refer to as learned helplessness. Why do students respond so differently to the same failure experience? Consistent with Weiner's attributional analysis, Dweck claims that learned helplessness in achievement situations occurs when students perceive failure to be insurmountable. When failure is perceived in this way, it often results in seriously impaired performance. In contrast, positive achievement behavior, which is Dweck's mastery-oriented attributional style, tends to attribute failure to factors that are within the individual's control, particularly insufficient effort.

It has also been shown that helpless students are more likely than mastery-oriented students to make their attributions spontaneously (Licht & Dweck, 1984). For example, when helpless students confront difficulty, they tend to focus attention on their past failure and their inability to overcome failure. In contrast, when mastery-oriented students confront obstacles, they tend not to contemplate the causes of their difficulties nor even the fact that they are having difficulty, but instead focus attention on strategies for solving the problem (Diener & Dweck, 1978).

Like attribution and learned helplessness, self-efficacy is another heuristic construct used by researchers to identify the learning difficulties of low achievers. Self-efficacy refers to a student's self-perception of possessing the prerequisite ability to be effective (Bandura, 1977). A student who lacks self-efficacy believes that no amount of effort will bring about a positive outcome. Self-evaluative or metacognitive techniques have been used successfully with low achievers to promote an attitude of self-efficacy and to reveal and reshape attributions (Brainin, 1985).

Self-confidence is related to a distinction Nicholls (1979) makes between task orientation and ego orientation. When task-oriented, the student's attention is focused on the process of completing the task; when ego-oriented, attention is focused on the self and especially on external evaluations of self. This distinction is illustrated in interview data reported by Peterson and Swing (1982). When questioned about her thoughts during a probability lesson, task-oriented Jani responded by describing the strategies she had used to solve the problem. Ego-oriented Melissa, however, discussed her nervousness and fear of undertaking the assignment. She summarized her thoughts by saying, "Well, I was mostly thinking . . . I was making a fool of myself" (p. 486). Clearly, Melissa's attention was on herself and not on completing the task.

The problems associated with ego involvement become more serious with age. Youngest children uniformly have an exaggerated perception of their own abilities and perceive effort and ability to be psychologically equivalent (Covington, 1984; Stipek & Hoffman, 1980). It is at about age eight that children begin to identify their own self-worth (Harter, 1983), and approximately one year later they can realistically compare their competence with that of others (Ruble, 1983). Then, beginning in grade six students perceive that ability closely reflects actual performance (Nicholls, 1978). Finally, as students enter junior high school, they can fully understand the reciprocal nature of ability and effort. This final revelation is a major turning point in the school careers of some low achievers, because they now perceive effort as a major cue for judging inability (Covington, 1984, p. 15). Thus, many of these older students opt to exert little or no effort to avoid being perceived as lacking ability.

Gender also appears to be related to continued motivation and task persistence. Research has shown that girls tend to have unduly low expectancies (Eccles, 1986; Smey, 1980; Stipek & Hoffman, 1980), to avoid challenge (Licht, Linden, Brown & Sexton, 1984), to focus on ability attributions for failure (Licht & Shapiro, 1982; Nicholls, 1979), and to exhibit debilitation under failure (Licht & Dweck, 1984; Licht, Linden, Brown & Sexton, 1984). In an interesting study, Licht and associates (1984) compared boys and girls with high grade point averages and found that girls much preferred tasks at which they could succeed, whereas boys preferred tasks at which they would have to work hard to master. These researchers conclude that boys are more likely than girls to prefer academic areas such as mathematics, which tend to necessitate surmounting difficulties at the beginning of new units. Other researchers (e.g., Ryckman & Peckham, 1987) have also found that girls demonstrate a more learned helplessness orientation in mathematics and science than do boys.

CULTURAL DIFFERENCES

Although the focus of this resource document is on low achievers, in general, research indicates that there are perceptual, cognitive, and behavioral differences among racial and ethnic groups that contribute to low achievement in minority students. Research on perceptual differences has focused on minority students' ability to structure information visually or to select and use relevant information embedded in a larger interrelated context (Witkin, Dyk, Paterson, Goodenough & Karp, 1962). After considering some evidence to the contrary, Shade (1982) suggests that Black students (Barclay & Cusumano, 1967; Gilbert II & Gay, 1985; Hale, 1982; Hilliard, 1976; Jones, 1978; Perney, 1976) and Hispanic students (Ramirez & Price-Williams, 1974) demonstrate a field-dependent preference (i.e., are unable to distinguish necessary parts to solve a problem), whereas white students demonstrate a field-independent preference (i.e., are able to abstract necessary parts from the totality of the material, regardless of distracting elements). When field-dependent/independent students are compared in terms of their scholastic achievement, regardless of sex or race/ethnicity, field-dependent students are poorer readers (Stuart, 1967; Zamm, 1973), take longer to master a reading-type task (Peterson & Margaro, 1969), and perform poorly in the school setting (Coop & Sigel, 1971; Kogan, 1971).

Witkin and Goodenough (1977) investigated the relationship between perceptual style (i.e., field dependent/independent) and personality style. They found that field-independent individuals tend to be impersonal or less interested in people, whereas field-dependent individuals demonstrate a preference for interpersonal relationships. Consistent with these findings, others have shown that Blacks – who tend to be field dependent – are person- rather than object-oriented, socially interactive, and prefer a cooperative rather than a competitive environment (Boykin, 1979; Gilbert II & Gay, 1985).

In addition, other researchers report that Blacks process information differently than whites. For example, Hilliard (1976) found that Blacks prefer intuitive rather than inductive or deductive reasoning and approximate rather than exact concepts of space, number, and time, as well as relying on nonverbal communication more than oth-

11

ers. As a possible explanation for these differences, Young (1974) suggests that Black children are taught by their parents to concentrate on many stimuli at one time rather than learning to concentrate on only one. Boykin (1979) refers to this as "behavioral verve." He found that when presented with information requiring some type of problem-solving preference, Black children did markedly better if the task format had high variability. From this, Boykin concludes that white students are socialized to tolerate monotony or unvaried presentation of material, whereas Black students require a great variety of stimuli.

Many educational researchers have compared Black and white students in terms of their self-esteem. Studies predating the 1960s generally found Blacks to have lower self-esteem than whites (for a review see Dillard, 1983; Ockerman, 1979), but more recent studies show that Blacks have a self-esteem equal to or higher than that of whites (Bowler, Rauch & Schwarzer, 1986; Hoelter, 1983; Jones, 1979; Porter & Washington, 1979). DeVos (1984) explains this recent dramatic increase in Black self-esteem as a reaction to past caste inferiority, increased militancy, and an interest in African heritage. In contrast, Hoelter (1983) attributes the change to "selective credulity" or the tendency of Black students to permit only the favorable appraisals of significant others to impact on their self-assessment. Others have also shown that Black students tend to disregard negative feedback from whites because it is not perceived as being objective (Banks, Stitt, Curtis & McQuater, 1977).

Studies of self-esteem in Hispanics indicate that a lower self-evaluation is found more often among the moderately acculturated (e.g., second- and third-generation) than among the least (e.g., first-generation) and most acculturated (e.g., fourth-generation). For example, Dworkin (1965) found that first-generation Mexican-American adults demonstrated a more favorable self-image than did second and third-generation Mexican American adults who experienced stress as a result of trying to adjust to the Anglo-American culture. Also, Knight, Kagan, Nelson, and Gumbiner (1978) found similar generational trends in the self-esteem of school-age Mexican Americans.

One widespread notion commonly reported in the literature is that Black children have a more external locus of control than white children, and, specifically, are more likely to attribute achievement outcomes to luck (e.g., Coleman et al., 1966; Frieze, 1981; Lefcourt, 1966; Murray & Mednick, 1975; Nowicki & Duke, 1974). However, in a recent study of approximately 400 Black, Hispanic, and white students in grades four to eight, Willig, Harnisch, Hill, and Maehr (1983) found that luck attributions did not emerge as a distinguishing factor for Blacks when compared with the other two ethnic groups. They also found that Blacks were least likely to attribute failure to task difficulty and/or lack of ability, whereas Hispanics tended to attribute failure to lack of ability. It is interesting to note that Black and Hispanic students who were in the process of moving up the socioeconomic status scale or of becoming acculturated to the Anglo-American life style were most influenced by debilitating motivational variables, including a low self-concept of academic ability and high anxiety in relation to school performance.

A number of educators have observed that the cultural values of Asians are a crucial element in their amazing educational success. The results of a recent study (Ginsburg & Hanson, 1986), based on a sample of nearly 12,000 disadvantaged sophomore students included in the 1980 High School and Beyond (HSB) survey, show that a similar association between superior academic success and student cultural values also applies to Black, Hispanic, and white students from low SES families. That is, high achievers among all racial and ethnic populations were found to be more likely than low achievers to believe they control their own fate, to work hard in school, to think it pays to plan ahead, to have a mother who thinks they should attend college, and to have friends in school who think well of students with good grades. Moreover, longitudinal data from the 1982 HSB follow-up survey indicate that initial student values significantly affect student outcomes, thus confirming the causal order assumed in the study.

Negative peer pressure may be another factor influencing Black and other minority students to perform below their tested ability levels (Snider, 1987). Based on interviews with Black high school students, researchers (Fordham & Ogbu, 1987; Ogbu, 1986; Petroni, 1970) have found that excelling in an arena seen as dominated by white values and expectations puts Black students in jeopardy of being accused of "acting white." These students view academic success

13

as part of the white value system and, hence, intentionally "put the brakes on" their school work to avoid ostracism from their peers and the Black community. Some highly successful Black students develop elaborate coping mechanisms that deflect attention away from their academic achievements. These mechanisms include emphasizing athletic achievement, acting like the "class clown," forming alliances with bullies, and sharing tests and homework answers with less successful peers.

Research shows that some Hispanic subgroups are also alienated from the traditional school culture. In an ethnographic study of a Californian high school located in an agricultural/suburban community, Matute-Bianchi (1986) found that approximately half of the Mexican-descent students, (i.e., the most alienated Mexican-oriented students, who call themselves "Chicano") rejected the behavioral and formative patterns required for scholastic achievement, e.g., participating in class discussions, carrying books from class to class, asking the teacher for help in front of others, and expending effort to do well in school (also see Farias, 1973). As it is not possible or legitimate for these students to participate in both the dominant school culture and the Chicano culture, they must choose between the two. Matute-Bianchi further explains:

> To cross these cultural boundaries means denying one's identity as a Chicano and is viewed as incompatible with maintaining the integrity of a Chicano identity. Hence, school policies and practices are viewed as forces to be resisted, subverted, undermined, challenged, and opposed. Often the opposition takes the form of mental withdrawal, in which the students find themselves alienated from the academic content of the school curriculum and the effort required to master it (p. 255).

Finally, some observers suggest that minority students fail to reach their full potential in the traditional American school because the educational environment is not only unresponsive to their needs, but also opposes their learning and interpersonal styles (Gilbert II & Gay, 1985). Boykin (1980) supports this position when he states that although Black children are eager to learn when they first come to school, they soon become uninterested by the educa-

14

tional process "when confronted with artificial, contrived and arbitrary competence modalities (e.g., reading and spelling) that are presented in ways which undermine the children's cultural frame of reference" (p.11). Proponents of this viewpoint call for a multicultural/multiethnic curriculum (Gay, 1979; Gilbert II & Gay, 1985; Sizemore, 1979) and teaching strategies that are matched to students' cognitive styles (Boykin, 1979; Gilbert II & Gay, 1985). Although there is strong evidence that differences in cognitive style are related to racial/ethnic group membership, there are virtually no research studies on multicultural education (Sleeter & Grant, 1987) and little is known about whether adopting alternative teaching styles or multicultural/multiethnic curricula will enhance the learning and performance of low achievers (Frechtling, 1984).

TEACHING IMPLICATIONS

Thus far, this resource document has described select student characteristics that differentiate the learning involvement of low-achieving students from that of their more successful peers. To summarize, low achievers not only tend to have poorer cognitive abilities, but also to lack an active and persistent approach to problem-solving. In addition, these students experience repeated failure that seriously erodes their belief in themselves and their ability to control academic performance. These two factors – poor cognitive ability/skills and low self-concept – often combine to produce seriously impaired learners who perceive failure to be insurmountable (Dweck, 1976) and who believe that no amount of effort will bring about a positive outcome (Bandura, 1977).

This section of the resource document moves beyond describing factors that contribute to low achievement to a review of a variety of approaches that researchers and practitioners recommend for transforming low achievers into competent, involved learners. It consists of four parts: first, an overview of metacognition and strategies for facilitating student metacognitive behavior; second, a review of successful affective strategies; third, a description of both extrinsic and intrinsic strategies that have been found to motivate the slow learner; and fourth, an explanation of cooperative learning methods designed to change classroom goal structures that negatively affect low achievers.

METACOGNITION

Metacognition takes place when individuals are aware of the strategies they use in their own thinking. Osborn, Jones, and Stein (1985) refer to metacognition as "individuals' knowledge of, and control over their own thinking and learning" (p. 11). Other researchers have suggested that metacognition involves "the ability to know what we know and what we don't know" (Costa, 1984, p. 57) as well as the capacity to know what to do when we are unsuccessful (Armbruster, Echols & Brown, 1983).

Presseisen (1985) conceptualizes metacognition as having two dimensions. The first dimension – monitoring task performance – requires learners to watch their own activities by keeping place, sequencing, detecting and correcting errors, and pacing work. These monitoring activities result in a greater efficiency of performance. The second dimension – selecting and understanding appropriate strategies – requires the learner to focus attention on what is needed to solve a particular problem, to relate what is known to what must be learned, and to test the effectiveness of a strategy. In contrast to the first dimension's efficiency, these strategies provide power for completing the thinking processes.

In an effort to identify the basic characteristics of effective thinking in a wide variety of learning situations, some researchers (e.g., Brown, 1978; Sternberg, 1986a; Stice, 1987) have attempted to isolate behaviors that appear to lead to effective problem solving. Known as "executive functions," these higher-order processes orchestrate and direct other cognitive skills. Paris, Cross, and Lipson (1984), for example, suggest the following three executive functions:

- **Planning,** probably the major component of metacognition, refers to selecting a goal, developing a strategy to achieve the goal, and allocating time/effort to maximizing the task solution.

- **Regulation,** (other authors call this "checking" or "monitoring") refers to the ability to follow one's chosen plan and to monitor it effectively. It also includes the wisdom to decide if a new plan is needed or if it is better to persevere on the chosen path.

- **Evaluation** of person, task, and strategy variables refers to the assessment of task difficulty and the assessment of the relative effectiveness of different strategies within a problem-solving context. Evaluation is measured against a standard such as effort, ease, or certainty (p. 1241).

Improving Metacognition of Low Achievers

The first section of this resource document suggested that low-achieving students tend to be deficient in metacognitive skills and strategies. Specifically, low achievers are lacking in the self-direction of their learning. They do not adequately plan, regulate, or evaluate their academic activities. This situation is especially alarming as metacognition is now viewed as central to the development of skillful thinkers (Presseisen, 1987, p. 34). In addition, the competencies for learning how to learn have been described by some as having the most enduring effect on student achievement (Chipman & Segal, 1985).

What can be done to improve the metacognition of low-achieving students? Numerous studies and reviews have confirmed that specific learning skills can be taught directly (Anderson & Armbruster, 1984), whereas the executive functions are more difficult to impart and must evolve gradually over time (Gagne, 1980). Some supporters of this viewpoint maintain that low achievers, unlike their peers, need sustained, explicit skill instruction with much opportunity for practice and feedback (Campione & Armbruster, 1985; Jones, Palincsar, Ogle & Carr, 1987). Brophy (1986b) concurs when he writes that lower SES learners "need more structuring from their teachers, more active instruction and feedback, more redundancy, and small steps with high success rates" (p. 1073).

Research on the learning of skills offers some suggestions for teaching thinking skills directly. According to Beyer (1984b), any skill is learned best when the learners are:

- consciously aware of *what* they are doing, and *how* they are doing it [I would add also *why* they are doing it]

- not distracted by other inputs competing for attention

- seeing the skill modeled

- engaging in frequent, intermittent practice of the skill

- using feedback they received during this practice to correct their own performance of the skill

- talking about what they did as they engaged in the skill

- receiving guidance on how to use a skill at a time when they need the skill to accomplish a content-related goal

- receiving guided opportunities to practice the skill in contexts other than the one in which the skill was originally introduced (p. 558).

Closely related to the issue of how to improve metacognition is the question of whether thinking skills should be taught separately or as part of the regular curriculum. Jones, Palincsar, Ogle & Carr (1987) argue that low achievers need adjunct skill instruction with a strong emphasis on applying the new skills to the content areas. They believe a separate approach is necessary so that the intensive skills training does not interfere with content instruction. In contrast, others (e.g., Presseisen, 1987) stress integrating cognitive instruction into the regular school curriculum. One compromise position is the "incidental learning model," which provides for isolated strategy training followed by application in the actual learning environment (Derry, 1984). According to Derry and Murphy (1986), one advantage of this approach is that it engineers the gradual evolution of the important executive control functions that are so badly needed by the low achiever.

Finally, the role of the teacher in the classroom is another significant consideration when designing metacognitive instruction for low achievers. The movement to teach thinking emphasizes the teacher as planner and mediator of learning rather than as the traditional transmitter of knowledge (Cummins, 1986; Jones, Palincsar, Ogle & Carr, 1987; Presseisen, 1987). In this pedagogical framework, teaching has a dual agenda: first, teachers must consider the strategies that students need to learn the content; and second, they must determine how students can be helped to learn to use these strategies (Jones, Palincsar, Ogle & Carr, 1987, p. iiv). Thus, the teacher of the low achiever can be described as a unique combination of consultant (Hunkins, 1987), "classroom coach, gentle questioner, high motivator and steady guide" (Presseisen, 1987, p. 48).

The literature suggests that teachers can use a variety of specific strategies to enhance metacognition, independent of grade level and subject area. A few of these generalizable strategies identified by Costa (1984) and others are described below.

Reading to learn. Studying – learning from reading – is probably the most important set of metacognitive skills a student can acquire from school (Armbruster & Anderson, 1981). Unfortunately, most low-achieving students – especially Blacks and Hispanics (Engs, 1987) – fail to comprehend much of what they read. To improve comprehension, some investigators recommend that instruction should engage poor readers in specific activities before, during, and after reading. Jones (1985) presents the following typical repertoire of recommended strategies for each stage of reading along with selected references:

- **Before reading,** a reader should focus on linking new information to prior learning and on predicting the contents of the test. Strategies include, for example, mentally reviewing previously acquired information, skimming, making hypotheses and predictions, self-questioning, and prelearning new vocabulary.

- **During reading,** a reader attempts to refine earlier predictions by determining what is important or unimportant, clear or unclear. Depending on the purpose, strategies include, for example, generative underlining (Richards & August, 1975), inferring the main idea (Wittrock, 1984), elaborating the text, forming analogies (Sternberg, 1977), and answering questions associated with the text (Brown & Palincsar, 1982).

- **After reading,** if the information is to be learned, a reader might outline or summarize the text, look back to check for mislearnings, or reread what was unclear (Winograd, 1984).

Thinking aloud. The method of thinking aloud to compare problem-solving processes of low and high achievers was referred to in the first section of this resource document. Using this technique, researchers have found that successful students differ from unsuccessful ones in the extent to which they think about a problem, in their system of thinking, and in their ability to follow through on the process.

Thinking aloud is now being advocated as an effective teaching strategy to help low-achieving students develop a greater awareness of their own cognitive processes (Scardamalia & Bereiter, 1983) and to improve their problem-solving ability (Beyer, 1984a; Whimbey,

1984). Whimbey and Lochhead (1983) suggest that students work in pairs, with one member of each pair talking through a problem while the other checks for accuracy and keeps the problem-solver verbalizing his or her thoughts. Requiring students to describe their thoughts while thinking seems to stimulate more thinking. It also focuses attention on the process of arriving at the solution, rather than just on the correct answer.

Thinking aloud can be used during whole group instruction. The teacher can invite low-achieving students to think aloud as they solve a problem or, after the problem has been solved, to verbally review the procedures followed. Such attention to clarification helps students to re-examine their own problem-solving processes, to identify their errors, and to correct themselves (Costa, 1984).

Planning strategies. Typically, low achievers do not actively plan an appropriate problem-solving strategy. They tend to rely on a limited amount of information and frequently guess to solve a problem.

This problem suggests that before any learning activity, teachers should identify strategies and steps for approaching problems, rules to remember, and directions to follow. These guidelines help low-achieving students follow any of several optional processes and give the students a standard by which to judge their performance (Costa, 1984). During the learning activity, teachers should ask students to use the talk-aloud strategy to share the processes they used and to define alternative pathways. After the learning task has been completed, the students should focus attention on how well the rules were followed, how productive the strategies were, and whether more efficient alternative strategies should be used in the future.

Generating questions. Regardless of the subject area, it is useful for low-achieving students to pose study questions for themselves before beginning a new learning experience. Student-formulated questions activate prior knowledge and assist the learner in systematically focusing on important aspects of a relatively unfamiliar topic.

In addition to creating their own questions, Hunkins (1987) advocates that students be taught how to classify and analyze these questions they pose for themselves. For example, students can be provided with formal instruction on types of questions – perhaps a brief version of Bloom's *Taxonomy of Educational Objectives* (1956) – with sample questions under each category (Hunkins, 1987). By being able to judge if a question is of a lower or higher order, low-achieving students can better regulate their own cognition.

Paraphrasing or reflecting back. Inviting students to restate, translate, and compare each other's ideas causes them to become better listeners to their own thinking and to others' thinking (Costa, 1984, p. 61). Examples of ways to facilitate paraphrasing might be to say: "What I hear you saying is..." or "Let's reexamine Tom's suggestion for a minute."

Simulations and role playing. Role playing can improve the metacognition of low achievers, as assuming the role of another individual requires the player to consciously display the basic characteristics of that person. Dramatization serves to develop a hypothesis or prediction of how that person would react to others and to the situation itself (Costa, 1984, p. 61). Assuming the role of another person also can serve to reduce the ego-centered perception that some researchers believe is characteristic of the low achiever.

Modeling. Of all the instructional techniques suggested, modeling probably has the greatest influence on the metacognitive behavior of low-achieving students (Costa, 1984). As students learn by imitating, the teacher who demonstrates metacognition will probably produce students who are metacognitive. Examples of ways in which teachers can demonstrate metacognitive behavior include sharing their planning (e.g., describing their instructional goals and rationale for selecting these goals); revealing specific instructional strategies (e.g., classifying and labeling questions, defining the meaning of a concept); labeling their own metacognitive processes and those of their students (e.g., "What I am doing or you are doing now is making a plan of action."); and admitting that they do not know an answer and discussing alternative ways to produce that needed answer.

SUCCESS, EFFORT, AND FAILURE

Throughout the years, psychologists have noted the key role played by affect in the intellectual functioning that underlies learning. Piaget (1962, p. 130) observed, "We must agree that at no level, at no stage, even in the adult, can we find a behavior or a state which is purely cognitive without affect nor a purely affective state without a cognitive element involved." Based on the interactive relationship between affect and cognition, it would seem that an intervention designed to improve the academic performance of low achievers must also support the student's feeling of competence.

Research discussed in the "Review of the Problem" section of this document suggests that students' perceptions of the causes of their successes and failures influence their future achievement. Success enhances self-perceptions of competence only if the learner accepts responsibility for that success. Generally, people motivated to approach success tend to attribute their successes to ability and their failures to lack of effort. In contrast, failure-avoiding people tend to ascribe success to external factors such as luck or task difficulty and to attribute failure to inability.

It has been said that success breeds success, presumably because success also breeds a sense of self-worth. However, the complex relationship between success and the learner's interpretation of success raises many questions: To optimize learning, how successful must a low achiever be? How much effort should students be expected to exert in achieving success? And what role should failure play in producing a sense of self-confidence in the slow learner?

Brophy (1983, p. 203) contends that learning proceeds optimally when it involves continuous progress achieved through small, easy steps with consistent success along the way. He believes that low-ability students should be responding correctly to teacher questions at least 80 percent of the time; in seatwork assignments on which students are working independently, success rates should reach the 90-95 percent level (Brophy, 1982, p. 27).

Success at novel and challenging tasks is important to low achievers (Gagne, 1980), but overly difficult tasks produce confusion and discouragement. According to Brophy (1983, p. 203), the degree of cognitive strain produced by tasks that allow students a 50 percent or less success rate is so great that it exceeds the tolerance level of the slow learner. In this regard, Harter (1978) has shown that students feel motivated when they experience success with what they perceive as reasonable effort, but are discouraged when they achieve success only with sustained effort.

So far, we have seen that effort is an important perceived causal factor in achievement, and for the successful learner it is an important source of self-pride. Ironically, however, too much effort can put a student at risk. Kun and Weiner (1973) conclude that the combination of high effort and failure is especially damaging, as it leads to suspicion of low ability. It is this self-realization of incompetency that triggers humiliation and shame (Covington & Omelich, 1979b). Thus, writes Covington (1984):

> *Effort becomes a double-edged sword; students must exert some effort to avoid teacher punishment and personal feelings of guilt, but not so much effort as to risk incompetency-linked humiliation should they try hard and fail anyway (p. 10).*

However, effortless learning or the lack of failure can also present problems. Dweck (1975) concluded that continued success on easy tasks is ineffective in producing challenge-seeking and persistent behavior. Similarly, Meyer (1982) found that consistently easy tasks lower self-confidence. In addition, when tasks are too easy, students can become dependent on easy success to feel smart (Brown, Palincsar & Purcell, 1986, p. 126), and they will be inexperienced in dealing with the failures they will inevitably encounter (Dweck, 1975). Hence, work with low-achieving students should include practice and coping with failure, (e.g., Dweck, 1975). These students should also be taught that failure can be more beneficial than success if it is regarded as a source of information rather than as a threat. Indeed, successful students not only tolerate failure, they invite it.

Improving the Success of Low Achievers

The message to teachers is clear. In addition to ensuring that low-achieving students have a certain number of successful experiences, teachers must also help these students understand the relationship between their behavior and their performance. The performance of low achievers will be optimized when they accept responsibility for their successes, and when they understand that effort and persistence can overcome failure.

Dweck (1975, 1976) demonstrated that students' cognitions about the causes of success and failure can be altered through explicit teaching. She selected a sample of low-achieving students who exhibited learned helpless behavior in response to failure and randomly assigned them to one of two treatment groups: those receiving only success experiences, or those receiving attribution retraining. In the attribution retraining group, the experimenter explicitly attributed student failure to insufficient effort. After 25 daily lessons, both groups were retested for the effects of failure on their performance. Although no improvement was shown by the success-only training group, all of the students in the attribution retraining group showed an increased persistence after failure. Other researchers (e.g., Andrews & Debus, 1978; Fowler & Peterson, 1981) lend support to Dweck's finding that students can be trained to make effort attributions for failure and that such training will result in greater persistence in the face of failure.

Critics of attribution retraining caution that the focus on effort should not be to the exclusion of ability. Based on the finding that students much prefer to be seen as both able and hard working rather than just hard working (Covington & Omelich, 1979b), Brophy (1983) argues students should be taught that they have the ability to meet the demands made of them if they make reasonable, as opposed to maximal, effort to do so. In addition, Bar-Tal (1978) cautions that attribution retraining can perpetuate unrealistic self-perceptions. For example, if low achievers are in fact incapable of doing certain tasks (i.e., without necessary knowledge or skills), they should not be taught to expect they can perform them.

Mood management training, as developed by Meichenbaum (1977), is similar in some respects to attribution retraining practices. This type of training teaches students to monitor and control their own affective ideation during problem-solving situations. If, for example, a student is engaging in counterproductive statements about him/herself while studying, the individual is taught to change these covert negative statements to positive ones. Meichenbaum (1977) argues that negative ideation reflects an individual's "activated cognitive structure," which he defines as the processors that determine when to change, interrupt, or continue a thought. He speculates that, by rehearsing positive "self-talk" and other behaviors that are inconsistent with self-defeating attitudes, individuals can gradually evolve a cognitive structure that supports more appropriate behavior.

Based on the evidence suggesting that attributional patterns and self-defeating attitudes are changeable, it seems possible for teachers to succeed in changing maladaptive causal perceptions. Alderman (1986) proposed three instructional strategies for bringing about such change:

- **Establish proximal goals for students.** Proximal goals provide students with frequent feedback and success experiences.

- **Link effort to outcome.** Have students attribute success to effort (i.e., "I succeeded because I worked hard"); let them know how much effort and the kind of effort needed to complete the task.

- **Define ability as skill.** Teach students to think of ability in, for example, reading or writing as a skill that can be learned rather than as an ability which is intractable. Also, teach them the effective metacognitive strategies to help them become proficient in these skills (p. 13-14).

In addition to the strategies listed above, Brophy (1983) suggests that maladaptive causal perceptions can be changed in part if teachers assign low achievers appropriate learning tasks. Brophy defines appropriate as "offering the prospect of success with reasonable effort" (p. 208). If a task is too difficult, the instructional goal is not reasonably achievable, and the student will fail because of ability, not effort. Although this point may appear obvious, some researchers (e.g., Fisher et al., 1981) have found that it is common for low achievers to be assigned tasks that are too difficult for them. Without appropriate assignments based on a realistic assessment of a student's prior learning, there is no hope for creating positive student attitudes toward classroom tasks.

Two other variables, high expectations for achievement and a supportive school climate, have also been found to influence a student's sense of competence and self-worth. As each of these factors is covered in another resource document, it is sufficient to note here that a learning environment of mutual respect, trust, and caring is critically important to the intellectual development of the low achiever. Also significant are the teachers' high expectations for the academic performance of low achievers and the willingness of teachers to interact with low achievers in the same way as they do with high achievers. Without these classroom variables in place, any attempt to enhance the self-perceptions of the low achiever will be seriously limited.

MOTIVATION

The concept of student involvement in learning is closely related to that of academic motivation. A low-achieving student who appears to be uninvolved in learning is often labeled "unmotivated." Although the terms "unmotivated" and "motivated" commonly appear in discussions of student achievement, most authorities agree that motivation is an abstract concept that is not easy to define operationally. Wlodkowski (1986) refers to motivation as a term to explain *why* human behavior occurs. He defines motivation as:

> the word used to describe those processes that can (a) arouse and instigate behavior; (b) give direction or purpose to behavior; (c) continue to allow behavior to persist; and (d) lead to choosing or preferring a particular behavior (p. 6).

It is often useful to define motivation in relation to other factors and processes. Feather (1982), for example, conceptualized motivation as a product of two variables — expectancy and value. His theory posits that the effort students expend in reaching a particular goal is a function of, first, the degree to which they expect to be able to perform the task successfully if they apply themselves and, second, the degree to which they value participation in the task or the rewards that successful completion will bring. This theory assumes that both factors must be present for students to invest effort. It also implies that teachers must both help students to appreciate the value of academic activities and make sure that they can achieve success on these activities if they apply reasonable effort (Brophy, 1987).

Improving the Extrinsic Motivation of Low Achievers

To foster students' extrinsic motivation, rewards are used to induce learning. According to this approach, even if low-achieving students do not find a particular subject interesting, they may still be willing to learn to achieve the external reinforcers. Hence, extrinsic motivation emphasizes that the goal of the behavior, as opposed to the "doing" of the behavior, is the reason for the performance of behavior (Wlodkowski, 1986, p. 8). Consistent with this thinking, instructional strategies for supplying extrinsic motivation focus on linking successful task performance with desirable rewards.

In addition to grades, external rewards may include material rewards (e.g., prizes, consumables); activity rewards and special privileges (e.g., permission to play games, use special equipment, engage in self-selected activities); symbolic rewards (e.g., honor roll, honor society, display of good works); praise and social rewards (e.g., special attention from the teacher or peers); and teacher rewards (e.g., opportunities to do things with the teacher) (Brophy, 1987, p. 43).

In traditional classrooms, reward systems have little positive influence on the low achiever, as rewards are not only in short supply but also reserved for the brightest or the best. This shortage may force some low achievers to avoid success or to accept failure because of perceived lack of ability (Covington, 1984). One way to rectify this situation is to increase the number of available rewards and to make these rewards contingent on improvement over past performance or on the greatest achievement gain. Another approach is to use cooperative learning methods to focus attention on group rewards and achievement.

Brophy (1987) recommends that teachers offer and deliver rewards in ways that call attention to desired knowledge and skills rather than simply to the reward itself. Thus, an "A" can be given to provide the student with feedback about his/her skill attainment, but it should not be viewed as something of value in itself. Teachers should say, "You have an 'A' on your test, which shows that you master the new concepts" rather than, "Congratulations, you received the only 'A' in the class" (Stipek, 1982, p. 34). In addition, noncontingent rewards are not advisable. Rather, reinforcement should be contingent on specific, clearly defined accomplishments.

One common approach to fostering achievement is to present academic activities as instrumental to success in the future. Students are urged to master academic knowledge and skills because these can be used to meet the students' own current needs or to provide them with necessary prerequisites for social advancement. By portraying present school tasks as applicable to future goals, the teacher helps students view academic activities not as imposed demands to be resisted but as enabling opportunities to be valued.

Although making valued extrinsic rewards contingent on learning behavior can be an effective motivational strategy, some educators question its practice. One difficulty with extrinsic motivation is that learning may be seen only as a means to a more pleasurable end; that is, the reward may become more important than the learning (Grace & Buser, 1987). Another difficulty is that extrinsic motivation may be interpreted as bribing students to learn, which is inherently wrong. Some researchers believe that students will turn into "reinforcement junkies" who must have extrinsic incentives to learn (Wlodkowski, 1986). Finally, there is the concern that school structures establish false expectations of society, which seldom rewards individuals in direct relation to their deeds (Stipek, 1982).

Staw's (1976) review of research on motivation leads him to conclude that incentives can alter the direction and vigor of specific in-school behaviors (e.g., getting students to complete an assignment by a particular date). However, extrinsic rewards may also weaken a student's general interest in school learning and decrease voluntary learning that extends beyond the school. Several studies have yielded evidence suggesting that introducing an extrinsic reward for performing an already interesting task causes a significant decrease in intrinsic motivation (e.g., Daniel & Esser, 1980; Lepper, Greene & Nisbett, 1973). Similarly, Maehr (1976) found that although emphasis on external rewards may temporarily enhance performance, it may negatively affect continuing motivation by ruling out the establishment of more intrinsic task-related goals.

Improving the Intrinsic Motivation of Low Achievers

Intrinsic motivation refers to the pleasure or value associated with an activity itself. In intrinsic motivation, the "doing" of the behavior is considered to be the primary reason for the performance of that behavior (Wlodkowski, 1986, p. 8). Ideally, all students should be intrinsically motivated. They should want to study a subject for its own sake or for the sense of accomplishment it gives them.

Teachers can elicit intrinsic motivation by selecting academic activities that students will engage in willingly because they are interested in the content or enjoy the task. Brophy (1987) suggests that because teachers must work within the confines imposed by the nature of schooling (e.g., compulsory attendance, externally prescribed curriculum, mandatory evaluation systems), opportunities to motivate students are limited. In addition, students differ in what they find interesting and pleasurable. Nevertheless, teachers should strive to incorporate intrinsically rewarding activities into their instruction for low-achieving, noninvolved students.

One common sense notion supported by research is that students are more likely to persevere at a task which is, in itself, interesting to them (Story & Sullivan, 1986). Whenever curriculum objectives can be accomplished using a variety of activities, teachers should provide examples of people, places, or things germane to the youth culture or from current events. In addition to making subject matter interesting, teachers should also make learning relevant to the needs and goals of the student. Dull subjects will not seem dull when students can apply facts and formulas or information gleaned in class to personal problems or to their efforts to improve the quality of their daily lives.

Tasks also can be structured to induce interest in classroom activities. Techniques used to stimulate interest include providing elements of novelty and variety in learning activities; introducing dissonance or cognitive conflict; including imagination or fantasy, which engages students' emotions; and incorporating game-like features such as puzzles or brain-teasers (Brophy, 1987).

Researchers have demonstrated the importance of a sense of control in motivating students. Deci (1980) and deCharms (1976) stress that a person's behavior may be modified by his or her sense of initiating events rather than being controlled by them. In an attempt to reverse the desperate state of an inner-city school in which both teachers and students had little interest, deCharms (1976) taught students to think for themselves as determiners of their own behavior by emphasizing participation, choice, and freedom in the classroom. His efforts resulted in a perception of greater responsibility over learning, higher achievement scores, and a relatively high rate of high school graduation among low-income youth.

To tap the motivational effects of self-determination, teachers should offer students alternative ways to meet requirements and provide them with opportunities to exercise autonomous decisions in organizing their time and effort. Students who make poor decisions when left alone, should be made aware of their alternative choices, with the requirement that they obtain teacher approval before proceeding (Brophy, 1987).

Stinson (1984) concurs that students must take charge of their own learning to sustain academic achievement. To do so, he suggests the following steps be taken:

- The teacher selects the criteria for mastery.

- The teacher and student negotiate and agree upon goals for the student.

- The teacher ensures that instruction will be individualized in its effect.

- The teacher and student reach an understanding that criteria for evaluation will be based on the student's past performance in relation to learning goals.

- The teacher's evaluation is based on the comparison of the current level of the student's performance with the previous level of performance on similar tasks (p. 179).

Most low-achieving students are more challenged by and prefer learning activities that actively involve them. Rather than just passively listening, taking tests, and reading, low achievers should be provided with opportunities to interact with their teacher and each other, to manipulate materials, to develop projects, and to write reports and stories. They should also be expected to participate in experiments, research, role plays, simulations, educational games, and creative application of what they have learned (Brophy, 1987).

Low achievers, as compared with their other classmates, generally receive less frequent and qualitatively inferior feedback from their teachers. This is an important finding, as feedback appears to facilitate student motivation and subsequent performance. Immediate student awareness of progress usually serves as an incentive toward increased effort (Wlodkowski, 1986). To offer more immediate feedback, teachers can incorporate it into typical activities by leading the group through an activity and then circulating to monitor student progress during seatwork. Teachers can also arrange for alternate sources of feedback such as providing answer keys or instructions about how to check class work. In cooperative learning situations, students review answers and then provide feedback to their teammates. In addition, automatic feedback features are built into computerized learning programs and other types of programmed instruction.

Research also indicates that in elementary school reading classes low achievers are continuously drilled in pronunciation and decoding, whereas high achievers are questioned about the meaning behind what they are reading and are frequently asked to evaluate and criticize material (Brown, Palincsar & Purcell, 1986). Most low-achieving students become bored by a steady diet of drill and practice and by questions at the knowledge and comprehension level. Hence, teachers can improve low achievers' interest in instruction by including questions that address higher levels of cognition (Brophy, 1987).

COOPERATION VS. COMPETITION

Since the 1970s, there has been a growing interest in using principles of cooperation as a means of improving the academic performance of the low achiever. As a result, a wide variety of techniques, called cooperative learning methods, have been developed and evaluated in school settings (see Sharan, 1980; Slavin, 1980, 1983b). What characterizes these methods is that they allow students to work in small heterogeneous groups toward a common goal. The groups usually have four members — one high achiever, two average achievers, and one low achiever. The students in each group are responsible not only for learning the material being taught in class, but also for helping their teammates learn. Hence, an essential feature of cooperative learning methods is that the success of one student helps other students to be successful (Slavin, 1982, p. 6).

Of course, cooperative learning techniques are not new. Teachers have used them for many years in the form of laboratory groups, project groups, discussion groups, and other such collaborative methods. In addition to these informal types, however, several independent teams of researchers have carefully engineered and published the following six learning methods: Student Team-Achievement Divisions, Teams-Games-Tournaments, and Jigsaw II (Slavin, 1981, 1982); Jigsaw I (Aronson, 1978); Learning Together (Johnson & Johnson, 1975); and Group Investigation (Sharan & Sharan, 1976). All of these methods are generic forms of cooperative learning and are applicable across grade levels and subject areas. They can be used with many types of curricula and are intended to supplement instruction.

In contrast to the principles underlying cooperative methods, most American schools are characterized by a competitive learning mode (Levine, 1982) in which the likelihood of a given student achieving success is reduced by the presence of other able students (Slavin, 1987). Competitive practices, such as grading on the curve or determining the best performers, create a condition of having fewer rewards than there are players. As a result, a student's sense of self-worth becomes dependent on doing better than someone else (Covington, 1984).

The competitive goal structure appears to be especially damaging to the low achiever. Research has shown that for these students competition tends to magnify negative affects associated with failure, e.g., self-attribution of low ability, shame, and guilt (Ames & Felker, 1979), and that competition, as compared with cooperation, causes failing students to become more self-punishing and to perceive themselves as less capable (Ames, 1978, 1981). These conditions force some low achievers to adopt tactics designed to avoid failure rather than pursue success (Covington, 1984). In addition, as low achievers become increasingly alienated and develop strong anti-academic norms, many turn to delinquency or withdrawal as a means of maintaining positive self-esteem in what they perceive to be a hostile environment (Slavin, 1981, p. 655).

In cooperative groups that have successful outcomes, the negative self-evaluation of the low performer has been found to be alleviated (Ames, 1978; Ames, 1981). Ames and Ames (1984) hypothesize that this occurs because, in a cooperative setting, group outcome information is central to the process of self-evaluation and group members share rewards and punishments depending on group outcomes. As a result, group productiveness modifies upward or downward the self-perceptions of high and low performers. These researchers also suggest that group productiveness causes students to judge their own ability and deservingness as similar to that of other performers in the group.

One principal idea behind cooperative learning methods is that because the group is rewarded, peer norms will come to favor rather than oppose high achievement. This occurs because individuals who are working together toward a common goal are likely to encourage one another to do whatever helps the group to be rewarded (e.g., Slavin, 1984). Slavin (1983b) has shown that students who experience cooperative learning are much more likely than students in a control group to believe that classmates want them to work hard. Students' perceptions that other students want them to excel may be especially salient to low-achieving Black and Hispanic adolescents. As shown in the first section of this document, these minority students are strongly influenced by anti-academic peer norms.

In theory, group rewards based on group performance should create group norms favoring performance. However, a substantial body of research has established that two conditions must be present if cooperative learning is to enhance student achievement (Slavin, 1987). First, students must be working toward a group goal such as earning certificates or some other form of recognition. This is a necessary factor as positive effects of cooperative learning methods result not from cooperative group study but from the use of group rewards (Slavin, 1984). And second, success at achieving this goal must be based on the sum of the individual learning performances of all group members. This discourages cooperative teams from relying on the highest achieving student and discouraging participation from low achievers.

Positive Effects of Cooperation over Competition

According to Slavin (1982), cooperative learning has been quite effective in increasing student achievement. Studies of successful cooperative learning have taken place in urban, rural, and suburban schools, at grade levels from 2 to 12, and in all major subject areas (Slavin, 1987). Positive effects have been found on higher-order objectives, such as creative writing, reading comprehension, and math problem solving, as well as on basic skill objectives, such as language mechanics, math computation, and spelling (Slavin, 1981). In general, positive achievement effects have been equivalent for high, average, and low achievers; for males and females; and for students with various ethnic backgrounds (Slavin, 1981, 1982).

In a recent review, Slavin (1987) reported that of 38 studies comparing traditional methods with a particular form of cooperative learning (i.e., a method that provides group goals based on the learning of all members), 33 found significantly greater achievement for the cooperative classes, whereas only five found no significant difference. In contrast, when cooperative learning lacked group goals based on group members' learning, there were few positive achievement effects. For example, in language arts, no difference in achievement was found between the Johnson's Learning Together method and traditional methods, and in mathematics, students using traditional methods retained more than those in the cooperative learning group (Slavin, 1982).

Some research evidence suggests that students who prefer to cooperate learn best in cooperative programs, while other students who prefer to compete do best in competitive programs (Slavin, 1981, 1982). This observation is especially significant for Black and Hispanic low achievers, many of whom are more predisposed to cooperation than are white students. Evidence has also shown that Black students register outstanding gains as a result of working together (Lucker, Rosenfield, Sikes & Aronson, 1976; Slavin, 1977). In one study, Black students in a middle school English class made so much progress with cooperative learning that the traditional achievement gap between them and white students was eliminated (Slavin & Oickle, 1981). In another study, however, no positive achievement effects were found for Blacks (Slavin, 1979). When reviewing this literature, Slavin concluded that racial differences in the effects of cooperative learning on achievement remain a perplexing problem (Slavin, 1982, p. 22).

In addition to improving student achievement, cooperative learning methods have a positive effect on a young person's social development (Frechtling, 1984). In one of his many studies in this area, Slavin (1978) reported that team classes were on task more than nonteam classes and that students in team classes were more motivated, felt more peer support, perceived a greater probability of success, and named more classmates as friends than those in nonteam classes. Other variables that have been positively affected by cooperative learning include race relations, acceptance of mainstreamed academically handicapped classmates, student self-esteem, and student liking of class (Slavin, 1983a).

SUMMARY

This resource document is concerned with the involvement of low achievers in the learning process. Research has shown that low achievers not only tend to have poor cognitive ability, but also lack an active, tenacious approach to task performance. As a result, low achievers often experience repeated failures that negatively affect their self-concept and contribute to their belief that they have failed, not because of lack of effort, but because of lack of ability. Few experiences of success, along with attributing failure to inability, interact to produce the learned helpless student who perceives failure to be inevitable and adopts failure-avoiding rather than success-seeking strategies. By the time they reach high school, many of these low achievers become increasingly alienated from the school environment, and they either drop out before graduation or turn their interest elsewhere, such as to sports or delinquent activities.

Implicit in this resource document is the belief that intelligence is modifiable and that low achievers at all grade levels can be motivated to work toward excellence. This is not to say that it is easy to convince students who have fared poorly in school for many years that they can succeed with effort. However, research has shown that in an environment in which independent, self-directed learning is encouraged and individual student competition is deemphasized, skilled teachers can be effective in reintroducing low achievers to the pleasures of learning.

The recommendations presented for enhancing low achievers' involvement in learning begin with a discussion of metacognitive strategies and skills. As low achievers generally are less able to select appropriate problem-solving strategies or to monitor their task performance, it is suggested that teachers directly teach low achievers how to be aware of their own thinking strategies. To enhance metacognition, low achievers might learn, for example, appropriate study skills (e.g., how to learn from reading); thinking aloud problem-solving methods; and planning, self-questioning, and paraphrasing techniques.

Any intervention designed to improve the academic performance of low achievers will succeed only to the extent that it supports the student's feeling of competence. Therefore, it is also recommended that students be taught to accept responsibility for their success and to understand that effort and persistence can overcome failure. Attribution retraining practices and mood management training are two techniques researchers have successfully used to show that self-defeating attitudes of low achievers are changeable. Classroom teachers interested in adjusting maladaptive causal perceptions of low achievers might, for example, establish proximal goals with many opportunities for success and feedback, encourage students to attribute success to effort, and instruct them to think of ability as a changeable rather than intractable characteristic.

Researchers and practitioners have found that extrinsic motivation can be used to induce low-achieving students to learn by linking successful task performance to desirable rewards. Others, however, criticize the use of rewards, as extrinsic motivation has been found to weaken general interest in learning and to decrease voluntary learning that extends beyond the school. Ideally, therefore, teachers should aim at intrinsically motivating the low achiever to study a subject for its own sake and for the sense of accomplishment such study affords. Instructional strategies that foster intrinsic motivation include building interest and active participation into learning tasks, encouraging low achievers to make autonomous decisions, providing immediate feedback to student responses, and asking higher-order thinking questions.

In exploring the tendency of low achievers to possess self-defeating attitudes, some researchers report that the competitive goal structure of the traditional classroom is especially damaging to the self-concept of these students. As a result, there has been burgeoning interest in the use of cooperative learning methods as a means of improving the academic performance of low achievers. Research has shown that negative self-evaluation of low performers is alleviated in cooperative groups with successful outcomes. In addition, evidence suggests that cooperative learning methods may be especially beneficial to the academic achievement of Blacks and Hispanics, as these students are more peer-oriented and more predisposed to cooperation than are whites. Other positive outcomes of cooperative learning for low achievers include higher self-esteem, a perceived greater probability of success, a greater student liking of the class, and an increased feeling of peer support.

The recommendations made in this resource document are not exhaustive and are not intended to serve as prescriptions, but rather as guiding principles to assist teachers in making instructional improvements to benefit the low achiever. The combination of strategies a teacher ultimately uses will depend on the unique strengths and teaching style of the teacher as well as the age level and other distinguishing characteristics of the students. To ensure that the strategies used are also effective, teachers must experiment with and evaluate their selected methods within the context of the classroom.

Finally, some of these recommendations are not easily implemented. Most require skill and dedication on the part of teachers, and some may require teacher inservice training and coaching. In addition, teachers' high expectations and a school environment supportive of change are critical. It is also hoped that teacher efforts to improve the education of low-achieving students are fully encouraged and supported by building-level and central office administrators.

SAMPLE EDUCATION PROGRAMS

The literature on student involvement in learning includes many specific strategies and programs that may be effective for low-achieving youth. Examples of programs relevant to student involvement in learning are:

- Cooperative Integrated Reading and Composition (CIRC)
- Higher Order Thinking Skills (HOTS)
- Learning to Learn (LTL)
- Prevention of Academic Failure
- Team Accelerated Instruction (TAI).

A brief overview of each of these programs follows. The overviews are based primarily on written descriptions disseminated by the program developers.

COOPERATIVE INTEGRATED READING AND COMPOSITION (CIRC)

AUDIENCE: Reading and language arts students in upper elementary school, especially low achievers.

DESCRIPTION: Cooperative Integrated Reading and Composition (CIRC) is a comprehensive program for teaching reading and writing in grades 3 through 5.

Much as in traditional classrooms, teachers use basal readers and reading groups. However, students in this program are also assigned to teams consisting of two pairs of students, each pair from a separate reading group. The teams devote most of their time to working in pairs on a series of cognitive activities while the teacher works with one of the reading groups. The team activities include reading to one another; predicting narrative story outcomes; summarizing stories; writing responses to stories; and practicing spelling, decoding, and vocabulary. Students also work together determining main ideas and other comprehension skills.

During language arts instruction, a structured program based on a writing process model is used. While in their teams, students review each other's writing samples and prepare for publication of team books. Lessons on writing skills are fully integrated into students' creative writing. The program sequence of CIRC activities begins with teacher instruction followed by team practice, team pre-assessments and, finally, a quiz.

Certificates are given to teams based on the average performance of all team members on all reading and writing activities.

EFFECTIVENESS: In comparison with a control group, substantial positive effects of CIRC have been found on standardized tests of reading comprehension, reading vocabulary, language expression, language mechanics and spelling. The CIRC classes gained 30 to 70 percent of a grade equivalent more than control classes on these measures. Writing samples were also significantly improved (Slavin, 1987).

COSTS: For each classroom set, reading materials cost $75 and language arts materials cost $35. Two days of training are required at the rate of $400 per day per participant.

CONTACT:
Dr. Robert E. Slavin
Elementary School Program Director
Center for Research on Elementary and Middle Schools
Johns Hopkins University
3505 N. Charles Street
Baltimore, MD 21218
(301) 338-8249

HIGHER ORDER THINKING SKILLS (HOTS)

AUDIENCE: Originally designed for Chapter I students in grades 3-6; HOTS is also appropriate for other elementary students in grades K-6.

DESCRIPTION: The basic goal of the HOTS program is to enhance the student's ability to think through the use of computer-involved thinking activities. Measurable improvement in the basic skills and social confidence occurs indirectly from improvement in general problem solving ability rather than from direct instruction, drill, and practice.

HOTS students generally work in computer labs. The curriculum consists of teacher-student dialogues organized into a series of lesson plans. The lessons are structured around commercially available software for Apple IIe or GS. The activities, curriculum, and recommended teaching techniques are based on information processing theories of cognition, and focus on developing problem-solving skills related to organizing information and linking new information to existing ideas. The program can be used in conjunction with a school's existing curriculum, textbooks, and instructional approach.

EFFECTIVENESS: After one year of use, evaluation results show substantial gains on standardized tests in both reading and mathematics. An increase in self-confidence and articulation ability was also found for Chapter I students in a wide variety of ethnic and racial groups (Pogrow, 1987).

COSTS: Although curriculum materials are self-explanatory, a number of workshops are available depending on how HOTS is being used. For example, a one-week workshop is available to train Chapter I teachers. Cost for this week-long training is typically $300 per participant. In addition, cost for software varies from $40 to $300 per disc and the program's first year of curriculum materials is $73.95 per school. There is also a second year charge of $200 for Chapter I sites. This fee includes a second year of curriculum materials, update on all materials, and a subscription to the program's newsletter.

CONTACT:
Dr. Stanley Pogrow
University of Arizona
College of Education
Tucson, AZ 85721
(602) 621-1305

LEARNING TO LEARN (LTL)

AUDIENCE: Low-achieving junior and senior high school students needing improvement in basic skills and reasoning skills; and educationally disadvantaged college students.

DESCRIPTION: The objective of the Learning to Learn (LTL) program is to teach low-achieving students to become independent learners in all academic courses. The LTL approach was developed with the intention of introducing learning gains more rapidly and of benefiting students on a long-term basis by improving their learning strategies.

A group of Michigan researchers translated the learning behavior of successful students into a series of exercises that less successful students could apply directly to their academic work. These successful behaviors include breaking down major tasks into smaller, comprehensible units; generating questions from instructional materials; devising informal methods to assess progress; and identifying instructional objectives to direct study behavior.

This program is divided into three stages. First, the students learn to build general learning skills and subject-specific skills into their daily school work; second, they adapt these skills to their coursework; and third, they discover personal variations of these skills. The skills become second nature to the students after a few months. LTL is available to schools through a combination of workshops on the skills and instructional materials.

EFFECTIVENESS: Initiated in 1979, the program has proven to have positive, long-term effects on students' grade point averages, credits completed, retention in school, scores on competency exams, and advancement to post secondary schools. As a result of the program, students become more engaged in their classwork, more highly motivated and more frequent participants. The increased student motivation and improved performance has been shown to have a positive effect on teacher morale.

COST: The cost for training and all materials used during the training is $500.

CONTACT:
Val Christie
Learning Associates
129 Mount Auburn Street
Cambridge, MA 02138
(617) 354-8393

PREVENTION OF ACADEMIC FAILURE

AUDIENCE: Students performing below the fiftieth percentile on a standardized reading test (Gates-MacGinitie Reading Inventory) in grades K-2.

DESCRIPTION: The primary goal of the Prevention of Academic Failure Program is to prevent low-achieving students from experiencing failure in basic skills acquisition. The program is designed to improve student achievement while simultaneously improving their perceptions of school, themselves, and their teachers. The program gives teachers more of an opportunity to make professional decisions regarding the instruction of students by reducing the use of the referral system as a necessary solution to a child's academic problems.

School staff are organized into two clinical teams that include reading specialists, learning disabilities specialists, aides, case workers, undergraduate and graduate student teachers, and all K-2 teachers. Each team is headed by a teacher-leader, who is trained in group decisionmaking through the "quality circles" technique. Use of a team approach allows for instruction on a one-to-ten ratio or less. Each team plans and provides its own instruction, lasting two to three hours each day. Low achievers may receive additional instruction of three hours per day for four weeks during the summer.

EFFECTIVENESS: The program was initiated in the summer of 1985 with three pilot schools. By fall 1986, all of the entering second graders were at grade level and the test scores for the three pilot schools were higher than the six control elementary schools. The smaller teacher-student ratio promoted greater instructional flexibility, better identification of student needs, more direct instruction at individual levels, peer tutoring, improved self-esteem, and improved motivation.

COSTS: Approximately $250,000 was allocated by the Board for the summer program including transportation, teacher-leader training, and teacher salaries. Chapter I and TELLS funds assisted in support of the program. Reading specialists were reassigned from middle schools.

CONTACT:
Dr. William Beighan, Superintendent
West Chester Area School District
829 Paoli Pike
West Chester, PA 19380
(215) 436-7100

TEAM ACCELERATED INSTRUCTION (TAI)

AUDIENCE: Low-achieving mathematics students in grades 3-6, or older students not ready for a full algebra course.

DESCRIPTION: Team Accelerated Instruction (TAI) combines cooperative learning techniques with individualized instruction. The goal of the program is to entirely replace traditional instructional methods with a comprehensive cooperative learning method that prepares group members to succeed on individual assessments.

Based on results of a placement test, students enter an individualized mathematics sequence and proceed at their own pace. Teammates check each other's work and help with problems. However, final unit tests are taken without teammate help to assure individual accountability. On a weekly basis, teachers total the number of units completed by all team members and give certificates or other rewards to teams that exceed a criterion score.

The cooperative nature of the program permits the teacher to spend less time on managing the flow of materials and marking exercises and more time actually teaching students. The teacher's class time is devoted primarily to presenting lessons to small groups of students from various teams who are at the same point in the mathematic sequence.

EFFECTIVENESS: Studies have shown substantially greater learning of mathematics computations using the TAI program. TAI classes gained an average of twice as many measures of computation as traditionally taught control classes. After one year, these differences were smaller, but still substantial (Slavin, 1987).

COSTS: The Charge for the one-day required training is $400 plus expenses. In addition, each set of classroom materials costs $400.

CONTACT:
Dr. Robert E. Slavin
Elementary School Program Director
Center for Research on Elementary and Middle Schools
Johns Hopkins University
3505 N. Charles Street
Baltimore, MD 21218
(301) 338-8249

REFERENCES

Alderman, M. K. (1986). Teaching low-achieving students: Motivation for success. Focus, 12(2), 11-15.

Ames, C. (1978). Children's achievement attributions and self-reinforcement: Effects of self-concept and competition reward structure. Journal of Educational Psychology, 70(3), 345-355.

Ames, C. (1981). Competitive versus cooperative reward structures: The influence of individual and group performance factors on achievement attributions and affect. American Educational Research Journal, 18(3), 273-287.

Ames, C., & Ames, R. (1984). Goal structures and motivation. Elementary School Journal, 85(1), 39-52.

Ames, C., & Felker, D. W. (1979). Effects of self-concept on children's causal attributions and self-reinforcement. Journal of Educational Psychology, 71(5), 613-619.

Anderson, L. (1981). Short-term student responses to classroom instruction. Elementary School Journal, 82(2), 97-108.

Anderson, L. (1984). The environment of instruction: The function of seatwork in a commercially developed curriculum. In G. Duffy, L. Roehler, & J. Mason (Eds.), Comprehension instruction: Perspectives and suggestions (pp. 93-103). New York: Longman.

Anderson, L., Brubaker, N., Alleman-Brooks, J., & Duffy, G. (1984). Making seatwork work (Research Series No. 142). East Lansing: Michigan State University, Institute for Research on Teaching.

Anderson, T. H., Armbruster, B. B. (1984). Studying. In D. Pearson, R. Barr, M. Kamil, & P. Mosenthal,

Handbook of reading research (pp. 657-679). New York: Longman.

Andrews, G. R., & Debus, R. L. (1978). Persistence and the causal perception of failure: Modifying cognitive attributions. Journal of Educational Psychology, 70(1), 154-166.

Armbruster, B. B., & Anderson, T. H. (1981). Research synthesis on studying skills. Educational Leadership, 39(2), 154-156.

Armbruster, B. B., Echols, L. H., & Brown, A. L. (1983). The role of metacognition in reading to learn: A development perspective. Urbana: University of Illinois, Center for Studying of Reading.

Aronson, E. (1978). The jigsaw classroom. Beverly Hills, CA: Sage Publications.

Ausubel, D. (1964). How reversible are the cognitive and motivational effects of cultural deprivation? Urban Education, 1(1), 16-38.

Bachman, J. G., O'Malley, P. M., & Johnston, J. (1978). Adolescence to adulthood: Change and stability in the lives of young men. Ann Arbor: University of Michigan, Institute for Social Research.

Bandura, A. (1977). Self-efficacy: Toward a unifying theory of behavioral change. Psychological Review, 84(2), 191-215.

Banks, W. C., Stitt, K. R., Curtis, H. A., & McQuater, G. V. (1977). Perceived objectivity and the effects of evaluative reinforcements upon compliance and self-evaluation in Blacks. Journal of Experimental Social Psychology, 13(5), 452-463.

Barclay, A., & Cusumano, D. R. (1967). Father absence, cross-sex identity and field dependent behavior in male adolescents. Child Development, 38(1), 243-250.

Bar-Tal, D. (1978). Attributional analysis of achievement-related behavior. Review of Educational Research,

48(2), 259-271.

Beal, P. E., & Noel, L. (1980). What works in student retention: The report of a joint project of the American College Testing Program and the National Center for Higher Education. (ERIC Document Reproduction Service No. ED 197 635.)

Bereiter, C., & Englemann, S. (1966). Disadvantaged children in the preschool. Englewood Cliffs, NJ: Prentice-Hall.

Beyer, B. K. (1984a). Improving thinking skills – defining the problem. Phi Delta Kappan, 65(7), 486-490.

Beyer, B. K. (1984b). Improving thinking skills: Practical approaches. Phi Delta Kappan, 65(8), 556-560.

Birch, H., & Bortner, M. (1970). Cognitive capacity and cognitive competence. American Journal of Mental Deficiency, 74(4), 735-744.

Bloom, B., & Broder, L. (1950). Problem solving processes of college students. Chicago: University of Chicago Press.

Bloom, B. S. (Ed.) (1956). Taxonomy of educational objectives. New York: McKay.

Blum, M. E., & Spangehl, S. D. (1982). Developing education programs for the high-risk secondary school and college student. Urban Diversity Series, 80. New York: Columbia University, Institute for Urban and Minority Education.

Bowler, R., Rauch, S., & Schwarzer, R. (1986). Self-esteem and interracial attitudes in Black high school students. Urban Education, 5(1), 3-19.

Bowles, S., & Gintis, H. (1976). Schooling in capitalist America. New York: Basic Books.

Boykin, A. W. (1979). Psychological/behavioral verve: Some theoretical explorations and empirical manifestations. In A. W. Boykin, A. Franklin, & J. Yates

(Eds.), Research directions of Black psychologist (pp. 351-366). New York: Russell Sage Foundation.

Boykin, A. W. (1980). Reading achievement and the social cultural frame of reference of Afro-American children. Paper presented at NIE, Roundtable Discussion on Issues in Urban Reading, Washington, DC.

Brainin, S. S. (1985). Mediating learning: Pedagogic issues in the improvement of cognitive functioning. In E. W. Gordon (Ed.), Review of research in education (pp. 121-155). Washington, DC: American Educational Research Association.

Bronfenbrenner, U. (1975). Is early intervention effective? Some studies of early education in familial and extrafamilial settings. In A. Montagu (Ed.), Race and IQ (pp.114-144). New York: Oxford University Press.

Brophy, J. E. (1982). Fostering student learning and motivation in the elementary school classroom. East Lansing: The Institute for Research on Teaching, Michigan State University. (ERIC Document Reproduction Service No. ED 225 584.)

Brophy, J. E. (1983). Conceptualizing student motivation. Educational Psychologist, 18(3), 200-215.

Brophy, J. (1986a). Socializing student motivation to learn. East Lansing: Michigan State University, Institute for Research on Teaching. (ERIC Document Reproduction Service No. ED 269 384.)

Brophy, J. (1986b). Teacher influences on student achievement. American Psychologist, 41(10), 1069-1077.

Brophy, J. (1987). Synthesis of research on strategies for motivating students to learn. Educational Leadership, 45(2), 40-48.

Brown, A. L., (1978). Knowing when, where, and how to remember: A problem of metacognition. In R. Glaser (Ed.), Advances in instructional psychology: Vol. 1 (pp. 77-165). New York: John Wiley & Sons.

Brown, A. L., Campione, J. C., & Day, J. D. (1981). Learning to learn: On training students to learn from texts. Educational Research, 10(2), 14-21.

Brown, A. L., & Palincsar, A. A. (1982). Introducing strategic learning from texts by means of informed self-control training. Technical Report No. 262. Urbana: University of Illinois, Center for the Study of Reading.

Brown, A. L., Palincsar, A. S., & Purcell, L. (1986). Poor readers: Teach, don't label. In U. Neisser (Ed.), The school achievement of minority children (pp. 105-143). Hillsdale, NJ: Lawrence Erlbaum Associates.

Bruner, J. S. (1959). Learning and thinking. Harvard Educational Review, 29(3), 184-192.

Campione, J. C., & Armbruster, B. B. (1985). Analysis acquiring information from texts: An analysis of four approaches. In J. W. Segal, S. F. Chipman, & R. Glaser (Eds.), Thinking and learning skills: Relating instruction to research: Vol. 1 (pp. 317-359). Hillsdale, NJ: Lawrence Erlbaum Associates.

Cattell, R. B. (1971). Abilities: Their structure, growth and action. Boston: Houghton Mifflin.

Chance, P. (1986). Thinking in the classroom. New York: Teacher College Press.

Chipman, S. F., & Segal, J. W. (1985). Higher cognitive goals for education: An introduction. In S. F. Chipman, J. W. Segal, & R. Glaser (Eds.), Thinking and learning skills: Vol. 2 (pp. 1-18). Hillsdale, NJ: Lawrence Erlbaum Associates.

Coleman, J. S., Campbell, E. Q., Hobson, C. J., McPartland, J., Weinfield, F. D., & York, R. L. (1966). Equality of educational opportunity. Washington, DC: U.S. Government Printing Office.

Coop, R. H., & Sigel, I. E. (1971). Cognitive style: Implicatives for learning and instruction. Psychology in the Schools, 8, 152-161.

Costa, A. L. (1984). Mediating the metacognitive. Educational Leadership, 42(3), 57-67.

Costa, A. L. (Ed.) (1985). Developing minds: A resource book for teaching thinking. Alexandria, VA: Association for Supervision and Curriculum Development.

Covington, M. V. (1984). The self-worth theory of achievement motivation: Finding and implications. Elementary School Journal, 85(1), 5-20.

Covington, M. V., & Omelich, C. L. (1979a). Are causal attributions causal? A path analysis of the cognitive model of achievement motivation. Journal of Personality and Social Psychology, 37(4), 1487-1504.

Covington, M. V., & Omelich, C. L. (1979b). Effort: The double-edged sword in school achievement. Journal of Educational Psychology, 71(2), 169-182.

Cummins, J. (1986). Empowering minority students: Framework for intervention. Harvard Educational Review, 56(1), 18-36.

Daniel, T. L., & Esser, J. K. (1980). Intrinsic motivation as influenced by rewards, task interest, and task structure. Journal of Applied Psychology, 65, 566-573.

deCharms, R. (1976). Enhancing motivation: Change in classroom. New York: Irvington.

Deci, E. L. (1980). The psychology of self-determination. Lexington, MA: D. C. Heath.

Derry, S. J. (1984, April). Strategy training: An incidental learning model for CAI. Paper presented at the annual meeting of the American Educational Research Association, New Orleans, LA. (ERIC Document Reproduction Service No. ED 247 884.)

Derry, S. J., & Murphy, D. A. (1986). Designing systems that train learning ability: From theory to practice. Review of Educational Research, 56(1), 1-39.

DeVos, G. A. (1984). Ethnic identity and minority status: Some psycho-cultural considerations. In A. Jacobson-

Widding (Ed.), Identity: Personal and socio-cultural. Uppsala, Sweden: Almquist & Wiksell.

Diener, C., & Dweck, C. (1978). An analysis of learned helplessness: Continuous changes in performance strategy and achievement cognitions following failure. Journal of Personality and Social Psychology, 36(2), 451-462.

Dillard, J. M. (1983). Multicultural counseling. Chicago: Nelson-Hall.

Doyle, W. (1982). Stalking the mythical student. Elementary School Journal, 82(2), 529-533.

Dweck, C. S. (1975). The role of expectation and attribution in the alleviation of learned helplessness. Journal of Personality and Social Psychology, 31(4), 674-685.

Dweck, C. S. (1976). Children's interpretation of evaluative feedback: The effect of social cues on learned helplessness. Merrill-Palmer Quarterly, 22(1), 105-109.

Dweck, C., & Bush, E. (1976). Sex differences in learned helplessness: Differential debilitation with peer and adult evaluators. Developmental Psychology, 12(2), 147-150.

Dweck, C., Davidson, W. S., Nelson, S., & Enna, B. (1978). Sex differences in learned helplessness: II. The contingencies of evaluative feedback in the classroom and III. An experimental analysis. Developmental Psychology, 14(2), 268-276.

Dweck, C., & Gilliard, D. (1975). Expectancy statements as determinants of reaction of failure: Sex differences in persistence and expectancy change. Journal of Personality and Social Psychology, 32(3), 1077-1084.

Dweck, C., & Goetz, T. (1978). Attributions and learned helplessness. In J. Harvey, W. Ickes, & R. Kidd (Eds.), New directions in attribution research: Vol. 2 (pp. 157-179). Hillsdale, NJ: Lawrence Erlbaum Associates.

Dweck, C., & Reppucci, N. (1973). Learned helplessness and reinforcement responsibility in children. Journal of Personality and Social Psychology, 25(1), 109-116.

Dworkin, A. G. (1965). Stereotypes and self-images held by native-born and foreign born Mexican Americans. Sociology and Social Research, 49(2), 214-224.

Eccles, J. S. (1986). Gender-roles and women's achievement. Educational Researcher, 15(6), 15-19.

Ekstrom, R. B., Goertz, M. E., Pollack, J. M., & Rock, D. A. (1986). Who drops out of high school and why? Findings from a national study. Teachers College Record, 87(3), 356-373.

Engs, R. G. (1987). Historical perspective on the problem of Black literacy. Educational Horizons, 66(1), 13-17.

Farias, Jr., H. (1973). Mexican-American values and attitudes toward education. In C. B. Allison (Ed.), Without consensus: Issues in American education (pp. 83-90). Boston: Allyn and Bacon, Inc.

Feather, N. (Ed.) (1982). Expectations and actions. Hillsdale, NJ: Lawrence Erlbaum Associates.

Feuerstein, R. (1980). Instrumental enrichment: An intervention program for cognitive modifiability. Baltimore: University Park Press.

Fisher, C., Berliner, D., Filby, N., Marliave, R., Cahen, L., & Dishaw, M. (1981). Teaching behaviors, academic learning time and student achievement: An overview. Journal of Classroom Interaction, 17(1), 2-15.

Fordham, S., & Ogbu, J. U. (1987). Black students' school success: Coping with the burden of "acting white." Urban Review, 18(3), 176-206.

Fowler, J. W., & Peterson, P. L. (1981). Increasing reading persistence and altering attributional style of learned helpless children. Journal of Educational Psychology, 73(2), 251-260.

Frankenstein, C. (1979). They think again. New York: Van Nostrand.

Frechtling, J. (1984). A review of programs and strategies used in other American school systems for improving student achievement. Rockville, MD: Montgomery County Public Schools. (ERIC Document Reproduction Service No. ED 255 584.)

Frieze, I. H. (1981). Children's attributions for success and failure. In S. S. Brehm, S. M. Kassin, & F. X. Gibbons (Eds.), Developmental social psychology, theory and research. New York: Oxford University Press.

Gagne, R. M. (1980). Learnable aspects of problem solving. Educational Psychologist, 15(2), 84-92.

Gardner, H. (1983). Frames of mind: The theory of multiple intelligences. New York: Basic Books.

Garrett, H. E. (1971). Heredity: The cause of racial differences in intelligence. Kilmarnock, VA: Patrick Henry Press.

Gay, G. (1979). On behalf of children: A curriculum design for multicultural education in elementary school. Journal of Negro Education, 48(3), 324-340.

Gilbert II, S. E., & Gay, G. (1985). Improving the success in school of poor Black children. Phi Delta Kappan, 67(2), 133-137.

Ginsburg, A. L., & Hanson, S. L. (1986). Values and educational success among disadvantaged students. Unpublished manuscript, U.S. Department of Education, Washington, DC (photocopy).

Glaser, R. (1976). Components of a psychology of instruction: Toward a science of design. Review of Educational Research 46(1), 1-24.

Gordon, E. W., with Green, D. (1975). An affluent society's excuse for inequality: Developmental, economic and educational. In A. Montagu (Ed.), Race and IQ (pp. 73-103). New York: Oxford University Press.

Gottfredson, D. C. (1980). Personality and persistence in education: A longitudinal study. Baltimore: Johns Hopkins University Center for Social Organization of Schools. (ERIC Document Reproduction Service No. ED 195 911.)

Grace, L., & Buser, R. L. (1987). Motivation. The Practitioner, Newsletter of the National Association of Secondary School Principals, 14(1), 1-12.

Hale, J. E. (1982). Black children: Their roots, culture and learning styles. Provo, UT: Brigham Young University Press.

Hall, E. (1982). Schooling children in a nasty climate: Interview with Jerome Bruner. Psychology Today, 16(1), 57-63.

Harter, S. (1978). Effectance motivation reconsidered: Toward a developmental model. Human Development, 21(1), 34-64.

Harter, S. (1983). The perceived competence scale for children. Child Development, 53(1), 87-97.

Hilliard, A. (1976). Alternatives to IQ testing: An approach to the identification of gifted minority children. Sacramento: California State Department of Education.

Hoelter, J. W. (1983). Factorial invariance and self-esteem: Reassessing race and sex differences. Social Forces, 61(3), 834-846.

Hunkins, F. P. (1987). Sharing our instructional secrets. Educational Leadership, 45(3), 65-67.

Jensen, A. R. (1969). How much can we boost IQ and scholastic achievement? Harvard Educational Review, 39(1), 1-123.

Johnson, D. W., & Johnson, R. T. (1975). Learning together and alone. Englewood Cliffs, NJ: Prentice-Hall.

Jones, B. F. (1985). Reading and thinking. In A. L. Costa (Ed.), Developing minds: A resource book for teaching thinking (pp. 108-113). Alexandria, VA: Association for Supervision and Curriculum Development.

Jones, B. F., Palincsar, A. S., Ogle, D. S., & Carr, E. G. (1987). Learning and thinking. In B. F. Jones, A. S. Palincsar, & D. S. Ogle (Eds.), Strategic teaching and learning: Cognitive instruction in the content area (pp. 3-32). Alexandria, VA: Association for Supervision and Curriculum Development.

Jones, E. E. (1978). Black-white personality differences: Another look. Journal of Personality Assessment, 42(3), 244-252.

Jones, E. E. (1979). Personality characteristics of Black youth: A cross-cultural investigation. Journal of Youth and Adolescence, 8(2), 149-159.

Kagan, J. (1975). The magical aura of the IQ. In A. Montagu (Ed.), Race and IQ (pp. 52-58). New York: Oxford University Press.

Knight, G. P., Kagan, S., Nelson, W., & Gumbiner, J. (1978). Acculturation of second- and third-generation Mexican-American children. Journal of Cross-Cultural Psychology, 9(1), 87-97.

Kogan, N. (1971). Educational implications of cognitive styles. In G. S. Lesser (Ed.), Psychology and educational practice (pp. 242-292). Glenview, IL: Scott, Foresman.

Kun, A., & Weiner, B. (1973). Necessary versus sufficient causal schemata for success and failure. Journal of Research in Personality, 7(3), 197-207.

Lefcourt, H. M. (1966). Internal versus external control of reinforcement: A review. Psychological Bulletin, 65(2), 206-220.

Lepper, M. R., Greene, D., & Nisbett, R. E. (1973). Undermining children's intrinsic interest with extrinsic reward: A test of the "over-justification" hypothesis. Journal of Personality and Social Psychology, 28(1), 129-137.

Levine, J. (1982). Social comparison and education. In J. Levine, & M. Wang (Eds.), Teacher and student perceptions: Implications for learning. Hillsdale, NJ: Lawrence Erlbaum Associates.

Licht, B. G., & Dweck, C. S. (1984). Determinants of academic achievement: The interaction of children's achievement orientation with skill area. Developmental Psychology, 20(4), 628-636.

Licht, B. G., Linden, T. A., Brown, D. A., & Sexton, M. A. (1984, August). Sex differences in achievement orientation: An "A" student phenomenon? Paper presented at the meeting of the American Psychological Association, Toronto, Canada.

Licht, B. G., & Shapiro, S. H. (1982, August). Sex differences in attributions among high achievers. Paper presented at the meeting of the American Psychological Association, Washington, DC.

Lucker, G., Rosenfield, D., Sikes, J., & Aronson, E. (1976). Performance in the interdependent classroom: A field study. American Educational Research Journal, 13(2), 115-123.

Maehr, M. L. (1976). Continuing motivation: An analysis of a seldom considered educational outcome. Review of Educational Research, 46(3), 443-462.

Matute-Bianchi, M. E. (1986). Ethnic identities and patterns of school success and failure among Mexican-descent and Japanese-American students in a California High school: An ethnographic analysis. American Journal of Education, 95(1), 233-255.

Meichenbaum, D. H. (1977). Cognitive behavior modification: An integrative approach. New York: Plenum Press.

Meyer, W. U. (1982). Indirect communications about perceived ability estimates. Journal of Educational Psychology, 74(6), 888-897.

Murray, S. R., & Mednick, M. T. (1975). Perceiving the causes of success and failure in achievement: Sex, race, and motivational comparisons. Journal of Consulting and Clinical Psychology, 43(6), 881-885.

Nicholls, J. (1978). The development of the concept of effort and ability, perception and academic attainment, and the understanding of difficult tasks require more ability. Child Development, 49(3), 800-814.

Nicholls, J. (1979). Conceptions of ability and achievement motivation: A theory and its implications for education. In S. Paris, G. Olson, & H. Stevenson (Eds.), Learning and motivation in the classroom (pp. 211-238). Hillsdale, NJ: Lawrence Erlbaum Associates.

Nowicki, S., & Duke, M. (1974). A preschool and primary control scale. Developmental Psychology, 10(6), 874-880.

Ockerman, J. D. (1979). Self-esteem and social anchorage of adolescent white, Black and Mexican American students. Palo Alto, CA: R & E Research Associates.

Ogbu, J. U. (1986). The consequences of the American caste system. In U. Neisser (Ed.), The school achievement of minority children (pp. 19-56). Hillsdale, NJ: Lawrence Erlbaum Associates.

Osborn, J. H., Jones, B. F., & Stein, M. (1985). The case for improving textbooks. Educational Leadership, 42(7), 9-16.

Paris, S. G., Cross, D. R., & Lipson, M. Y. (1984). Informed strategies for learning: A program to improve children's reading awareness and comprehension. Journal of Educational Psychology, 76(6), 1239-1252.

Pellicano, R. R. (1987). At risk: A view of "social advantage." Educational Leadership, 44(6), 47-49.

Perney, V. H. (1976). Effects of race and sex on field dependence-independence in children. Perceptual and Motor Skills, 42(3), 975-980.

Peterson, P. L., & Swing, S. R. (1982). Beyond time on task: Students' reports of their thought processes during classroom instruction. Elementary School Journal, 82(2), 481-491.

Peterson, P. L., Swing, S. R., Braverman, M. T., & Buss, R. (1982). Students' attitudes and their reports of cognitive processes during direct instruction. Journal of Educational Psychology, 74(4), 535-547.

Peterson, S., & Margaro, P. (1969). Reading and field dependence: A pilot study. Journal of Reading, 12(4), 287-294.

Petroni, F. A. (1970). "Uncle Tom:" White stereotypes in the black movement. Human Organizations, 29(4), 260-266.

Piaget, J. (1962). The relation of affectivity to intelligence in the mental development of the child. Bulletin of Menninger Clinic, 26(1), 129-137.

Pogrow, S. (1987). A thinking skills approach to using computers to improve the basic skills of at-risk students: Experience with the HOTS program. Tucson, AZ: College of Education, University of Arizona.

Porter, J. R., & Washington, R. E. (1979). Black identity and self-esteem: A review of studies of Black self-concept. In A. Inkeles (Ed.), Annual review in sociology (pp. 53-76). Palo Alto, CA: Annual Reviews, Inc.

Presseisen, B. Z. (1985). Thinking skills: Meanings and models. In A. L. Costa (Ed.), Developing minds: A resource book for teaching thinking (pp. 43-48). Alexandria, VA: Association for Supervision and Curriculum Development.

Presseisen, B. Z. (1987, November). Teaching thinking and at-risk students: Understanding the problem. Paper presented at the Cross-Laboratory National Conference, Research for Better Schools, Inc., Philadelphia, PA.

Ramirez, M., & Price-Williams, D. (1974). Cognitive styles of children of three ethnic groups in the United States. Journal of Cross-Cultural Psychology, 5(2), 212-219.

Rickards, J. P., & August, G. J. (1975). Generative underlining strategies in prose recall. Journal of Educational Psychology, 67(6), 860-865.

Rotter, J. (1966). Generalized expectancies for internal versus external control of reinforcement. Psychological Monographs, 1 (whole no. 609).

Ruble, D. N. (1983). The development of social comparison processes and the role in achievement-related self-socialization. In E. T. Higgins, D. N. Ruble, & W. W. Hartup (Eds.), Social cognition and social development (pp. 134-157). New York: Cambridge University Press.

Ryckman, D. B., & Peckham, P. (1987). Gender differences in attributions for success and failure situations across subject areas. Journal of Educational Research, 81(2), 120-125.

Scardamalia, M., & Bereiter, C. (1983). In S. G. Paris, G. M. Olson, & H. W. Stevenson (Eds.), Learning and motivation in the classroom (pp. 61-82). Hillsdale, NJ: Lawrence Erlbaum Associates.

Schwebel, M. (1968). Who can be educated? New York: Grove Press.

Shade, B. J. (1982). Afro-American cognitive style: A variable in school success? Review of Educational Research, 52(2), 219-244.

Sharan, S. (1980). Cooperative learning in small groups: Recent methods and effects on achievement, attitudes, and ethnic relations. Review of Educational Research, 50(2), 241-271.

Sharan, S., & Sharan, Y. (1976). Small-group teaching. Englewood Cliffs, NJ: Educational Technology Publications.

Sizemore, B. A. (1979). The four m curriculum: A way to shape the future. Journal of Negro Education, 48(3), 341-356.

Skeels, H. M., & Skodak, M. (1949). A final follow-up study of 100 adopted children. Journal of Genetic Psychology, 75(1), 85-125.

Slavin, R. E. (1977). Classroom reward structure: An analytic and practical review. Review of Educational Research, 47(4), 633-650.

Slavin, R. E. (1978). Student teams and comparison among equals: Effects on academic performance and student attitudes. Journal of Educational Psychology, 70(4), 532-538.

Slavin, R. E. (1979). Effects of biracial learning teams on cross-racial friendships. Journal of Educational Psychology, 71(3), 381-387.

Slavin, R. E. (1980). Cooperative learning. Review of Educational Research, 50(2), 315-342.

Slavin, R. E. (1981). Synthesis of research on cooperative learning. Educational Leadership, 38(8), 655-660.

Slavin, R. E. (1982). Cooperative learning: Student teams. Washington, DC: National Education Association.

Slavin, R. E. (1983a). Cooperative learning. New York: Longman.

Slavin, R. E. (1983b). When does cooperative learning increase student achievement? Psychological Bulletin, 94(3), 429-445.

Slavin, R. E. (1984). Students motivating students to excel: Cooperative incentives, cooperative tasks and student achievement. Elementary School Journal, 85(1), 53-63.

Slavin, R. E. (1987). Cooperative learning and the cooperative school. Educational Leadership, 45(3), 7-13.

Slavin, R. E., & Oickle, E. (1981). Effects of cooperative learning teams on student achievement and race relations: Treatment by race interactions. Sociology of Education, 54(3), 174-180.

Sleeter, C. E., & Grant, C. A. (1987). An analysis of multicultural education in the United States. Harvard Educational Review, 57(4), 421-444.

Smey, B. A. (1980). Social educators' perceptions of women in administrative roles and curriculum (Doctoral dissertation, Rutgers University). Dissertation Abstracts International, 41, 195A.

Snider, W. (1987, March 25). Negative peer pressure said to inhibit Black student achievement. Education Week, p. 14.

Staw, B. M. (1976). Intrinsic and extrinsic motivation. Morristown, NJ: General Learning Press.

Sternberg, R. J. (1977). Intelligence, information processing, and analogical reasoning: The componential analysis of human abilities. Hillsdale, NJ: Lawrence Erlbaum Associates.

Sternberg, R. J. (1986a). How can we teach intelligence? Educational Leadership, 42(1), 38-48.

Sternberg, R. J. (1986b). Intelligence applied. New York: Harcourt Brace Jovanovich.

Stice, J. E. (1987). Developing critical thinking and problem solving abilities. San Francisco: Jossey Bass.

Stinson, M. (1984). Research on motivation in educational settings: Implications for hearing-impaired students. Journal of Special Education, 18(2), 177-198.

Stipek, D. J. (1982). Motivating students to learn: A lifelong perspective. Washington, DC: National Commission Excellence in Education. (ERIC Document Reproduction Service No. ED 227 111.)

Stipek, D. J., & Hoffman, J. (1980). Development of children's performance-related judgments. Child Development, 51(3), 912-914.

Story, N. O., & Sullivan, H. J. (1986). Factors that influence continuing motivation. Journal of Educational Research, 80(2), 86-92.

Stuart, I. R. (1967). Perceptual style and reading ability: Implications for an instructional approach. Perceptual and Motor Skills, 24(1), 135-138.

Walters, J. M., & Gardner, H. (1985). The development and education of intelligences. In F. R. Link (Ed.), Essays on the intellect (pp. 1-21). Alexandria, VA: Association of Supervision and Curriculum Development.

Wehlage, G. G., & Rutter, R. A. (1986). Dropping out: How much do schools contribute to the problem? Teachers College Record, 87(3), 374-392.

Weiner, B. (1979). A theory of motivation for some classroom experiences. Journal of Educational Psychology, 71(1), 3-25.

Whimbey, A. (1984). The key to higher order thinking is precise processing. Educational Leadership, 42(1), 66-70.

Whimbey, A., & Lochhead, J. (1983). Problem solving and comprehension: A short course in analytical reasoning. Philadelphia: Franklin Institute Press.

Willig, A. C., Harnisch, D. L., Hill, K. T., & Maehr, M. L. (1983). Sociocultural and educational correlates of success-failure attributions and evaluation anxiety in the school setting for Black, Hispanic, and Anglo children. American Educational Research Journal, 20(3), 385-410.

Winne, P. H. (1985). Steps toward promoting cognitive achievements. Elementary School Journal, 85(5), 673-693.

Winne, P. H., & Marx, R. W. (1982). Students' and teachers' views of thinking processes for classroom learning.

Elementary School Journal, 82(2), 494-518.

Winograd, P. N. (1984). Strategic difficulties in summarizing texts. Reading Research Quarterly, 19(4), 404-425.

Witkin, H. A., Dyk, R. B., Paterson, H. F., Goodenough, D.R., & Karp, S. A. (1962). Psychological differentiation. New York: John Wiley & Sons.

Witkin, H., & Goodenough, D. (1977). Field dependence and interpersonal behavior. Psychological Bulletin, 84(6), 661-689.

Wittrock, M. C. (1984). Generative reading comprehension. (Ginn Occasional Reports). Boston: Ginn and Company.

Wlodkowski, R. J. (1986). Motivation. Washington, DC: National Education Association.

Young, V. II. (1974). A Black American socialization pattern. American Ethnologist, 1, 405-413.

Zamm, M. (1973). Reading disabilities: A theory of cognitive integration. Journal of Learning Disabilities, 6(2), 95-101.

Research for Better Schools (RBS),
a private, non-profit, educational
research and development firm, was
founded in 1966. Its sponsors include
many clients from the public and private
sector who support R&D projects that
meet their needs. RBS is funded by the
U.S. Department of Education to serve as
the educational laboratory for the Mid-
Atlantic region.

Using the expertise of some 50 staff
members, RBS conducts research and
policy studies on key education issues,
develops improvement approaches and
services for schools, provides consultant
services to state leaders, develops
products for special populations, and
participates in national networking
activities with other regional
laboratories to enhance the use of R&D
products and knowledge.

During the past 20 years, RBS has
developed extensive capabilities which
are available to all education
professionals in the form of practical,
research-based products and services.
This publication is one of the products of
RBS' R&D work. Related training and
technical assistance services also are
available. Your interest in RBS is
appreciated and your suggestions or
requests for information always are
welcome.